HOLINESS

and the Spirit of the Age

FLOYD McCLUNG

HARVEST HOUSE PUBLISHERS
Eugene, Oregon 97402

HOLINESS AND THE SPIRIT OF THE AGE

Copyright © 1990 by Harvest House Publishers
Eugene, Oregon 97402

Library of Congress Cataloging-in-Publication Data

McClung, Floyd
   Holiness and the Spirit of the age / Floyd McClung.
   ISBN 0-89081-790-1
   1. Holiness.   2. Moral conditions   I. Title.
BT767.M22   1990
234'.8—dc20   90-36387
                                             CIP

Printed in the United States of America.

Let not the wise man glory in his wisdom,
let not the mighty man glory in his might,
let not the rich man glory in his riches;
but let him who glories glory in this,
that he understands and knows me,
that I am the Lord who practice steadfast love,
justice, and righteousness in the earth;
for in these things I delight, says the Lord.

Jeremiah 9:23,24

Grateful Acknowledgments

Many thanks to Geoff and Janet Benge and to my dear wife Sally. They edited, typed, and helped me write this book.

I am indebted to Os Guinness for helpful conversations in Manila and Washington D.C. His social critique of American culture has been crucial to my thinking. His book, *The Gravedigger File*, is a prophetic voice crying in the wilderness.

Chuck Colson and Jerry Bridges' books on holiness and commitment have been a great help to me, not only in writing this book, but also in stimulating my desire for God.

It is a wonderful thing when a publisher and editor live out what an author feels called to write about. Publisher Bob Hawkins and Editor-in-Chief Eileen Mason at Harvest House have earned my love and respect. They are professional, personable, and godly. Thank you both!

Contents

To Joy Dawson and Gordon Fee—
two of my spiritual mentors
who have profoundly shaped my understanding
of the character of God and His Kingdom.
Every time I speak or write,
their influence on my life is passed on to others.

Part 1

A Nation
Possessed

—1—
Captives in a Gilded Cage

everal years ago, my wife Sally and I became exhausted from our work in the inner city. We realized we needed to get away for some rest, so we called a pastor friend in San Diego and asked if he could help us. Our friend contacted his brother who arranged for us to stay in Palm Springs, California, at a vacation home owned by a successful businessman.

When we arrived in Palm Springs we couldn't believe our eyes. This businessman didn't have just one vacation home, he had six of them whose backyards adjoined. He had torn down all the fences and converted the combined backyard space into a giant playground for his family and friends. There were five swimming pools, jacuzzis everywhere, a sauna, a ping-pong table, a putting green, and a volleyball court. Inside our home was a pool table and, of course, televisions galore!

We launched into our five-week stay in this vacation paradise enthusiastically. We took long walks in the desert, swam, played, and enjoyed the quiet and privacy.

Our bodies were refreshed and our spirits soared. To be honest, we loved it! I thought several times, "I could really get into this!"

After several weeks, however, I found myself fighting an uphill battle to stay spiritually alert. Even though I had plenty of time for leisure, finding time to pray became more and more difficult. The love relationship with Jesus I had worked so hard to cultivate was being torn to shreds. The quietness of my soul was being replaced by a clumsy, flabby spirituality. I was becoming spiritually obese. Here I was, a minister of the gospel, but my spiritual life was falling apart. I was rapidly losing touch with God's concern for the poor and needy of the world—and all the while I was enjoying myself immensely!

I was discouraged and confused. I knew God's Word well. Paul emphatically declared, "For sin shall not be your master, because you are not under law, but under grace" (Romans 6:14, NIV). Despite this great-sounding promise of victory, I had been captured by the culture I was called to serve.

I'm not saying it was a sin for us to rest, nor did I feel guilty about enjoying such a great vacation spot. There is nothing wrong with relaxing and enjoying life. But when relaxation and fun cause spiritual flabbiness, we are no longer living in holiness.

As I wrestled with my discouragement I had to ask myself, "Can I really live a holy life, victorious over sin, in a worldly setting?" With all my heart I desired to live an obedient, holy life; yet I was utterly defeated by the simple comforts of American culture.

My experience in Palm Springs taught me an important lesson: My desire to live a holy life was on a collision course with the unholy culture around me. Even though I grew up in a godly home and received wonderful Christian teaching, I found myself in a battle for my spiritual life during that vacation. Only by recognizing that I was in a battle and by consciously resisting the temptations around me was I able to put the Lord first. My five weeks of physical rest and spiritual wrestling in that little desert paradise was the launchpad for discovering and applying many of the lessons I share in this book.

Trapped in Hostile Territory

We live in a complex world and are surrounded by an ungodly culture. Our whole nation is like an enlargement of that backyard playground in Palm Springs. German sociologist Max Weber suggests that modern culture is like a beautiful, gilded bird cage. We are caught in it and we cannot escape. We are encircled by its ideas and ideologies, by its structures and systems. Our culture is essentially unsympathetic—sometimes even hostile—to all we are called to be and to do as Christians.

We become holy and righteous by obedient faith in Christ through His death and resurrection. We are called to live in holiness and obedience as an outworking of our true identity in Christ. Reduced to its simplest definition, holiness means to be separate from the world and its sin. In his book *The Practice of Godliness*, Jerry Bridges writes:

> To be God-like in our character, then, is first of all to be holy. The practice of godliness involves the pursuit of holiness because God has said, "Be holy, because I am holy" (1 Peter 1:16). Paul tells us that we have been called to a holy life; we have been redeemed for that purpose. Any Christian who is not earnestly pursuing holiness in every aspect of his life is flying in the face of God's purpose for saving them.[1]

But the world in which we live is not holy. It's unholy. And the surrounding culture which permeates our daily existence is not under the direction of the Spirit of God who indwells us. It is dominated by a spirit which is opposed to holiness and righteousness—what the Bible calls the spirit of the age.

This book is written to help believers understand the spirit of the age and its influence on our culture so we can choose to separate ourselves from it. If we don't understand the world we live in—at least in part—it will seduce us into its unholy lifestyle, as I so quickly discovered during my five weeks in Palm Springs. *Tragically, we can become unholy without ever making a conscious choice to be worldly!*

The spirit of this "present evil age" (Galatians 1:4) is the spirit of selfishness. Though it takes many forms, it boils down to one thing: me first. Call it what you like—self-fulfillment, pleasure, whatever. It is evil. Satan is seeking to destroy the church of Jesus Christ by turning our attention away from Him and toward ourselves.

The spirit of the age comprises both spiritual powers and cultural forces. Satan—active in our world through demonic influence—personifies the spirit of the age (Ephesians 2:2). He and his demonic hosts are the "principalities," the "powers," the "world rulers of this present darkness," and the "spiritual hosts of wickedness in the heavenly places" (Ephesians 6:12).

Satan has exploited the sinful, selfish choices of fallen people, which has resulted in the capture of cultural forces by demonic principalities. The "opportunities" Satan presents to us in our culture are the same ones he offered to Jesus on the pinnacle of the temple, the same old sins dressed up in new disguises. Gold, glory, and all that glitters will be ours. All we have to do is to bow down to Satan by unthinkingly enjoying the pleasures offered to us. In doing so, we acquiesce to the cultural forces which surround us. These forces are designed to undermine individuals, families, and churches and to keep us from being all God intends us to be. Tragically, the church in America is being deeply influenced—often without even realizing it—by a culture which has been captured by Satan.

The nature of evil has not changed since the Garden of Eden. Pride, selfishness, rebellion, and deceit still work their depraved charm deep in the human heart. But in the late twentieth century, evil in America has become so pervasive and so embedded in the structures and institutions of our society, that unless believers are alerted to the falleness of American life and thinking, they will thoughtlessly compromise themselves to worldliness. Satan is a deceiver. He appears as an angel of light. He not only tempts us directly with appeals to "the lust of the flesh and the lust of the eyes and the pride of life" (1 John 2:16), he also surrounds us with an ostensibly wonderful culture which he has subverted for his cause in all its dimensions.

Blatant evil alarms us. But when Satan rules a culture that champions freedom and democracy, a culture that was built on the aspirations of those seeking opportunity to worship as their consciences dictated, then he can tempt us through the niceness and normalcy of "the American way." Though the structures of our modern culture seem innocuous, insidious evil is inherent in their very nature.

A Rival for the Throne

The spirit of the age has raised up other gods which are being unwittingly served by believers as well as unbelievers. As a nation we have put our trust in modern-day idols such as unhindered economic growth and the good life. We have been seduced by Satan and have pledged our allegiance to pleasure and prosperity. We have given to the American dream a devotion which belongs only to God.

As a result of our idolatry a number of demonic powers have invaded our nation and gained a foothold in our culture. They appear so unobtrusive that most believers have been content to peacefully coexist with them. But these forces are at strident cross-purposes with the life of holiness to which we have been called. In Part Two of this book we will expose five prominent spirits of the age which are poisoning our culture and drugging believers into ineffectiveness: 1) *the good-life gospel*—expecting God to give us everything we want and think we need; 2) *individualism*—making personal comfort and pleasure a priority over serving others; 3) *consumerism*—associating success with the accumulation of goods; 4) *pluralization*—diluting moral absolutes and cluttering daily life with too many choices; 5) *secularization*—shoving God out of the center of daily life and relegating Him to the harmless periphery.

Has our national allegiance to self-fulfillment and its servant spirits satisfied our needs and solved our problems? Not in the least. As Bob Goudzwaard says, "Our solutions have turned against us.... They still alleviate poverty and disease, improve crops, develop faster means of transportation.... But the problems they leave in their wake are often more serious and more structural than the problems they solve."[2] In our pursuit of health, wealth, prosperity, happiness, and security we have created modern-day gods, and as we will see, these gods have betrayed us.

Biblical Holiness

The purpose of this book is not to pronounce the inevitable decline of American society. Rather, it is to sound an alarm that our surrounding culture, which was once rooted in Christian values, has turned against its Christian heritage and destroyed it.

Furthermore, I want to issue a sober warning to believers about the great difficulty of living a life of undefiled devotion to the Lord Jesus in a culture that is so committed to comfort and affluence. When does a Christian who lives *in* the world cross the line and become a person *of* the world? Does it happen when we compromise on R-rated movies? spend more weekends away than we spend in church? focus our energies on making more money to buy more things? Though there is no simple answer to this serious question, it is a question that must be asked continually by every true Christian. How each of us responds to these questions may determine the future of the church in America, and our own personal destiny.

Many Christians do care about Jesus, but they see no connection between their personal relationship with the Lord, their lifestyle, and what is happening in their community. Something is wrong when religion is increasingly popular but public morality is continually compromised. Sadly, many of us have learned to separate our spiritual life from our practical lifestyle. Our conscience has become little more than a mirror of the world around us. We have stopped hearing the convicting voice of the Holy Spirit.

Living a life of holiness frees us from the spirit of the age. Our personal spiritual life becomes integrated with our work, our friendships, and our community involvement. Our lives become *whole* and *holy*. When our lives are marked by holiness we learn how to slow down long enough for the Lord and for others. Yet this lifestyle of holiness eludes us behind the smoke screen of the ever-present temptation to the good life. By bowing to the spirit of the age we are being robbed of what will truly make life worth living. The quality of life we long for is only found in a holy life.

When we cross the line and become *of* the world, certain consequences are inevitable. Instead of having time for God's Word, prayer, and meaningful friendships, we are consumed with our own pleasures and lose control of the quality of our lives. Instead of engaging the forces of

Satan which are destroying people's lives through unrighteousness and injustice, we are swept up in the relentless
and unfulfilling drive to have more fun and make more
money. As a result, families are driven apart and churches
split. Satan overwhelms us with pressures and problems
and prods us to accept pseudospiritual solutions instead of
seeking God's will and God's way.

Perhaps my experience at Palm Springs reminds you
of something you are struggling with. Maybe your circumstances are similar, maybe they are a little different. We
all struggle with areas of compromise. For some it's pride,
for others it's overeating, for still others it's an uncontrollable temper. Perhaps for you it's envy, impatience, or a
lack of involvement in your neighborhood.

If we are to overcome the spirit of the age we must be
devoted to Jesus in our hearts and minds. We must do some
hard thinking, some Spirit-led analyzing of how the spirit
of this present evil age has taken hold of our culture and, to
a great extent, Christian institutions. Only then can we
see the way forward to loving God with all of our mind,
soul, body, and strength. Only then can we overcome the
crisis of character facing our nation.

We need to understand what it means to be whole,
holy Christians in our nation today. The lack of tough-
minded devotion to Jesus could cost us our integrity as
believers. It is not enough to decide we will withdraw into a
small, safe world of simple choices. The spirit of the age
wins one more victory when Christians isolate themselves
from the world so that they can be "unworldly."

—2—
A Crisis of Character

I t is clear that a crisis of immense proportions has emerged in the culture within which we are called to be holy. The greatest threat before us is no longer a Russian invasion or a nuclear holocaust. Neither should our greatest concern be a stock market crash or even the erosion of the ozone layer. The greatest challenge before us is not an external threat but an internal one: a crisis of character. We are now a nation where "the values that restrain inner vices and develop inner virtues are eroding. Unprincipled men and women, disdainful of their moral heritage and skeptical of truth itself, are destroying our civilization by weakening the very pillars upon which it rests."[1]

Newspapers are filled with reports of corruption in high places. Drug wars rage on our streets. Racial bigots send letter bombs to murder those they hate. Material affluence obsesses adults, youth, and children. Politicians and businessmen trade integrity for cash. Families are breaking up, parenthood is in peril, crime is on the rise, and our nation seems impotent to return to the moral foundations which made it great. The Christian character which once typified the culture that surrounds us is being sacrificed to selfish desires, to the god of this age.

Crisis in the Family

We are living through a period of historic change in the structure and function of the family. It is no longer held together by its members' common need for one another. Now it is pulled apart by obsessive personal devotion to such symbols of success as the car, the television, and the telephone—and all the aspirations for independence and privacy which come with them. The character of the American family is being eroded by the spirit of the age.

The traditional family—a working father, a mother at home, and their children—no longer exists as a major force in society. Only 27 percent of American families qualify as traditional. In place of traditional families are families of diverse styles and shapes: single-parent families, step-families, and nonmarital families.

Children are paying the price for their parents' confusion of priorities and lack of commitment. Two-thirds of all mothers are in the labor force, swelling the population of latchkey kids who come home after school to an empty house. Sixty percent of all marriages currently end in divorce, and one-third of all children born in the United States will live in a step-family before they are 18 years old. It is estimated that over 70 percent of all violent, impulse crimes in the United States are committed by children from single-parent families.

Children of divorced parents suffer confusion, guilt, and trauma. They tend to blame themselves for their parents' divorce, avoiding a more painful implication: "Mother and father don't love me enough to stay together."

Children of divorce grow up committed to being

uncommitted. Half of all 30-year-olds cohabit before marriage, and many assume that marriage won't work for the long haul. Studies now show that couples who cohabit before marriage are more likely to divorce than those who do not.

The crisis of the disjointed family has extended into our neighborhoods. The sense of community no longer happens spontaneously as a result of people living close to each other in a homogeneous setting. It's rare when a person has the time to get to know his neighbors. Who has the energy for community after commuting an hour each way to work day in and day out? It seems that the pressures and hectic pace of daily life force people to withdraw from each other in order to survive.

A Crisis of Morality

No institution is immune to the erosion of standards. Officials in the state of New York exhumed the bodies of 33 patients who died suspiciously at Good Samaritan Hospital. Richard Angelo, a male nurse working at the hospital, was convicted of killing four of the patients and sentenced to 50 years in prison. Police suspect that he killed all 33 of them. Was Angelo attempting to play God by putting people out of their misery? No, it was more macabre than that. Angelo told police that he secretly gave patients potentially lethal injections so he could heroically attempt to revive them and bolster his performance record!

The current AIDS epidemic in America reflects the widespread tragedy our land is experiencing as a result of its morality crisis. More Americans have died from AIDS than died in the Vietnam war. It is estimated that within four years there will be half a million cases of AIDS in the United States. While gay men and intravenous drug users have dominated the statistics of AIDS victims, it is sobering to note that teenagers now compose *the third highest risk group!*

New approaches to AIDS education are being tried against a backdrop of evidence that sexually active teens still use condoms only sporadically. A recent analysis by the U.S. Centers for Disease Control of blood samples collected from 40 urban hospitals revealed that 1 percent of all 15- and 16-year-olds tested were infected with the AIDS virus. Among 21-year-olds the infection rate approached 3 percent. Even in the cities which researchers describe as medium risk, such as Atlanta, Chicago, and Dallas, about 1 percent of the 21-year-olds are infected.

According to a blood sample survey conducted on 19 college campuses in the late '80s, one in 500 students, a total of 25,000 people, may be carrying the AIDS virus. It is not difficult to imagine what will happen to our nation if AIDS continues to spread through a promiscuous and irresponsible generation of sexually active teenagers who are being seduced by the spirit of the age.

Crisis in Government

Neither are government officials immune from the plague of immorality and selfishness which characterizes a culture that has sold out. Marion Barry, the former mayor of our nation's capital, was indicted for drug use. He once boasted of being the city's greatest lover. Pentagon excesses have produced the kind of corruption which priced government toilet seats at $635 and screwdrivers at $150 each. During the '80s the nation's attorney general was accused of bribe-taking and the Speaker of the House was forced to resign over conflict of interests. Congressmen turn out bloated budgets and commission expensive studies on such topics as "The Future of the Belgian Endive." St. Augustine aptly described a government devoid of character when he wrote, "What is the state without justice? A band of robbers."[2]

Many social critics and American voters question a

political process which has turned presidential and congressional elections into multimillion dollar media blitzes. "Sound bites" are now more important than soundly conceived political positions. Is it possible for men of moral character and leadership to enter into, much less survive, this bizarre process?

When we step back and contemplate the effect of the erosion of character on the family, the community, public and private morality, and our political institutions, we should be deeply concerned about the state of our nation. And we should be just as concerned about the impact of the spirit of the age on Christians and the church.

Are Christians Exempt from the Crisis?

Surely Christian leaders and the Christian church are exempt from the crisis of character which is corrupting America's families, neighborhoods, and government—or are we? Surely we're not being seduced by the spirit of the age—or are we?

Judging by the evidence, Christians are neither exempt from the national crisis of character nor impervious to seduction by the spirit of this evil age. Christian shepherds and members of the flock alike must awaken to the reality that we are vulnerable to being influenced by the evil personalities and cultural forces which hold our world in their grip. Indeed, whether we want to admit it or not, we are already influenced by them.

Seduced by Immoral Spirits

Although we may expect that Christian leaders and followers alike are models of moral purity in an immoral age, the evidence proves that even Christians are being seduced by evil, impure spirits. We're well acquainted with the admonition of Scripture to "cast off the works of darkness and ... make no provision for the flesh, to gratify its desires" (Romans 13:12,14). But we are having difficulty separating ourselves from a culture that is consumed by "the flesh."

For example, Christian youth are not immune to the plague of promiscuity which is sweeping through our teen-age population. One survey showed that 43 percent of Christian teenagers engage in sexual intercourse by age 18, and 65 percent participate in petting and fondling. Furthermore, American Christians and the world at large were stunned by revelations of hypocrisy in the lives of television evangelists. So many spiritual leaders have fallen morally in recent times that ordinary believers have become cynical and mistrustful.

I remember sitting with my 16-year-old daughter Misha and watching a televangelist speak to an audience of 1000 teenagers about the importance of sexual purity. Just a few months later it was revealed that while this man had been preaching to teenagers about keeping themselves sexually clean, he had been visiting prostitutes. I'll never forget Misha's reaction of anger and disappointment. I sat up till the late hours of the night talking and praying with her about how God would have us respond to this man. Though we did not know him, his actions profoundly affected our family.

Seduced by National Pride

An overemphasis on our nation's greatness has compromised our allegiance to Christ. Christians have become arrogant about America's greatness as a nation while blind to her desperate need for God. At the core of this arrogance is civil religion, that force in our culture which cherishes the religious aspirations of our founding fathers to an extreme. What's wrong with that, you ask? Nothing in itself. But in the extreme, American evangelicals assume that the United States enjoys "most favored nation" status with God. We are deluded into thinking that God blesses

America because we are a great nation instead of the opposite.

We wrongly assume that material prosperity is a sign of God's blessing, and anything which appears to threaten our prosperity is obviously evil. We mistakenly equate capitalism with Christianity and material prosperity with spirituality. By promoting the unequal marriage of material prosperity and the spiritual well-being of the nation in the minds of Christians, Satan has laid the axe to the root of biblical Christianity in America.

The nation of Israel suffered from the same delusion in the Old Testament. "Why would God want to judge us?" they cried to the prophets. "Our fields are ripe with grain, so God must be pleased with us!" It didn't seem to matter to them that they worshiped idols and used unbalanced scales in the marketplace. "We are blessed physically, so we must be blessed spiritually," they said.

But it certainly mattered to God, who ordained no such equation. Obadiah wrote God's response: "Behold, I will make you small among the nations, you shall be utterly despised. The pride of your heart has deceived you" (Obadiah 2,3).

It is particularly dangerous when a nation such as ours marries its physical prosperity to a sense of spiritual well-being. We confuse the American creed with the Apostles' Creed. America the beautiful is assumed to be America the blessed. When we assume the national order is undergirded unconditionally with a Christian base, the result is civil religion instead of biblical Christianity. American Christians make the mistake of confusing our national agenda with God's burden for the world.

Crisis at a Critical Hour

When believers are caught up in the deception of exaggerated national pride and enmeshed in moral impurity, the spirit of the age has more influence in the church than the Holy Spirit. At this point the church cannot be separated from the world because it is inexorably married to it through an unholy union.

This is especially tragic in view of the fact that, in one sense, we are presently living in the church's finest hour. There is rapid expansion of the church in Asia, Africa, and South America. There is renewal and awakening in Europe and North America. The simultaneous emergence of the church on every continent in great numbers has never happened before in church history. It would be a great shame if God's people in this nation missed their destiny because of moral softness and compromise.

There is a battle raging for the church in our nation. It's a battle between God's Spirit and the spirit of the age—and we play a major role in the battle. Our commitment to holiness—or lack of commitment—will determine if we will fulfill our destiny in God's plan for the world or be relegated to the sidelines of history because we succumbed to the spirit of the age.

—3—
Whose Problem Is It Anyway?

I bought a snack and looked for somewhere to sit in the overcrowded airport restaurant. The only empty seat I could see was across the restaurant at a table where a woman was sitting next to a small baby in a stroller. Two enormous carry-on bags were pushed under the table.

I approached her and asked if she minded my sitting in the vacant seat. "Not at all," she replied brightly as she reached down to move one of her bags so I could get my legs under the table. "Excuse the bags, but we're headed back to the South Pacific and we need to take so many supplies back with us. You never know what's going to be available when you get there."

"And what are you doing down there?" I casually inquired.

The woman's face lit up. "Well, my husband and I are missionaries, actually. We're going back to set up a model farm for the islanders and establish a study program based on the teachings of Prophet Bahaullah. Have you heard of the great prophet?" She asked with a smile.

I nodded, desperately rummaging through my jet-lagged mind to recall all I knew about the Bahai faith.

"He teaches hope for the world," she went on. "So many religions today are down on people. Most of them keep saying that the world will be a horrible place by the time Shantalla grows up." She reached over and stroked her baby's cheek with her finger. "But it won't be, you know. Bahaullah says the world will get better and better and that we have the ability to help ourselves and each other. Together we can build a beautiful world. Isn't that wonderful?"

I hummed noncommittally, thinking how best to answer her question. "Do the islanders embrace your teaching?" I probed.

"Oh yes, they think it's wonderful," she chuckled, "except for a few fundamentalist Christians. They just can't see it. Fortunately there aren't many of them on the island we're going to. Anyway, they have nothing better to offer except gloom and doom."

I was still pondering how best to respond to her "beautiful world" theory when she was distracted by a man standing in the doorway of the restaurant who was motioning to her with his hands. "That's my husband," she said. "Time to catch our flight. Nice talking to you." She stood, heaved the two carry-on bags over the stroller handles, and made her way out of the restaurant.

As I watched her go I was intrigued at how happy and confident she was that her child would grow up in a beautiful world where life would get better and better. I thought about her perception of fundamentalist Christians who see gloom and doom instead of the beautiful world ahead. What would I have said to this woman if our conversation hadn't been cut short? Does the human race really possess the ability to create an increasingly better world until it finally becomes a utopian society? Are Christians merely killjoys out to spoil a beautiful world? What do we have to offer in the face of such unashamed optimism?

The Tainted Optimism of the World

On the surface, a better world does seem possible when we consider the amazing technological advances which have been made this century. And scientific breakthroughs continue to occur, many of which hold the potential to end much of the suffering in our world. I read in one newspaper recently about a team of doctors from Guy's Hospital in London who performed the first heart operation on a live fetus in its mother's womb. A balloon the diameter of a small sewing needle was inserted into the baby's heart to open up a closed valve which otherwise would have killed the baby.

The article also told about a team of American doctors who had performed lifesaving lung surgery on an unborn child who was removed from the womb and returned there after the operation. It was the first successful operation of its kind. The baby was born three months later. Six months old when the article was written, the baby was still alive and doing well.

The newspaper also described a new process pioneered by physicians at Temple University which facilitates out-of-the-womb surgery. It involves the use of "liquid breath," inert chemicals which hold large amounts of respiratory gases. The use of liquid breath in the fetus enables doctors to mimic the conditions in the womb where the baby breathes amniotic fluid. The process greatly increases the survival chances of premature infants and pushes back the boundary of fetal viability, the point at which a baby born prematurely can survive outside the womb. In the future, breakthroughs like these are going to remove much of the trauma and suffering involved with premature deliveries and congenital defects.

But sadly, the same newspaper which carried these stories of wonderful medical breakthroughs carried another article about an unborn child which was anything but optimistic for the future. The story told of an 18-year-old man who was being tried for killing his unborn son. When his former fiancée, who was pregnant with his child, broke up with him, the man told her that if he couldn't have the baby, neither could she. He then punched her in the head, kicked and punched her in stomach, picked her up and body-slammed her, and smashed her face into the concrete. The baby died in the womb that same night from internal bleeding and bruises to the stomach, liver, brain, and spleen.

What a clear picture of the human dilemma! One page carries a story about the wonderful medical advances made by brilliant physicians which will reduce suffering and prolong life in unborn infants. But the next page paints the dark portrait of a man so enraged by the breakup with his fiancée that he willfully and deliberately beats her up in order to kill the unborn child she is carrying. Furthermore, while millions of dollars are being spent every year on neonatal research, hundreds of thousands of women selfishly abort their unborn children simply because they don't want stretch marks or because their untimely pregnancies will interfere with career advancement. This is not the evidence of a world which is getting better and better. This is the evidence of a society with a serious problem.

Another example of the selfishness which reflects the spirit of the age is the woman who did not want her baby because it had Down's syndrome. Here is part of the letter she wrote to her retarded one-year-old baby boy, David:

> Our decision to have you adopted was instantaneous with the diagnosis. Your father and I knew right away that we could not accept you for

what you were. You were not the boy your daddy could have taken fishing or cheered from the sidelines of the football field. You could not grow up and gain a university degree or become a lawyer or a computer engineer or an airline pilot. We had been cheated of a son.

The woman continued by describing her feelings as she turned David over to a foster mother for adoption:

I felt immensely relieved, immensely humble, but strangely not guilty. There has never been room for guilt. As far as your father and I were concerned we were dealing with a tragic and critical situation for which we had to create a plan of action. Plans need to be single-mindedly followed through.

In finishing her letter she writes:

Very soon I am going to have another baby. I have lived in fear and trepidation since this conception. You see, I know the risks now—that I have a 1:100 chance of having another Down's Syndrome child. I won't let that happen. All the tests suggest he is normal. His name is Ben. You will never know him. I don't know if we will ever tell him about you. There seems no reason. We have no place in our lives for a little boy called David. For a short time a baby wandered into our lives. And we loved him. Enough to let him go.[1]

Here is a woman articulately explaining that since her first son could not grow up to earn a university degree, she and her husband had decided to give him away. She, of course, was not about to repeat the "mistake" of giving birth to a retarded child, so she was tested during pregnancy to make sure her second son didn't have the same defect. She implies that had her second fetus been defective, he would not have lived to see the light of day. Abortion would have been his fate. But neither she nor her husband would allow their minds to run down the path of guilt. David was merely a "tragic and critical situation" for which they had to create "a plan of action." They don't even think they will tell their new son about his older brother. There is seemingly no need for him to know that his parents produced anything less than perfection.

If a child must be a potential university graduate in order to win his parents' acceptance and earn the right to stay in the family, is our world really getting better and better? No, despite our technological achievements the world is far from utopia because of a fundamental problem with every one of its inhabitants.

Selfishness: The Root of Our Problem

The Bible says that the world's problem lies within humankind. Selfishness provoked the man to beat up his former fiancée in order to kill his unborn son. Pride motivated David's parents to throw him away. Greed and lust for power are behind the crisis of character which plagues our families, our government, and our churches. The marred character of the human race is the cause of the jealousy, hatred, lying, stealing, maiming, and killing which is rampant in our culture. The Bible calls this condition sin, and it is the black heart of the spirit of the age.

Sin is an unpopular term in modern America. People feel uncomfortable when they hear it and say it. So the world has figured out other ways to explain society's root problem. Psychologists talk about abnormal behavior. Marxists call it a class struggle—at least they used to before the upheavals in Eastern Europe. Educational experts refer to it as ignorance.

New Agers dispose of sin through a handy little process called "rebirthing." The rebirthing experience is supposed to deal with all the negative input we've received from our parents, which they say is the root of all the problems we face in life. And if your parents didn't cause the problem, then it was the doctor who delivered you! As you spiritually regress to the womb (some fortunate souls even go back into their past lives!) and are rebirthed, you are set free from all the negative influences in your life, or so the rebirther, a kind of cosmic midwife, says. Of course, after the rebirth you have to pay the rebirther a hefty fee, which is likely to be the first negative experience of your rebirthed life!

While on a recent visit to New Zealand I read about a group in French Polynesia with yet another explanation for society's great problem. The group describes itself, almost unbelievably, as "a gathering of telepathically inspired researchers, creators, and spiritual adventurers living in a multidimensional paradise, preparing and realizing contacts with civilizations of the future." According to this group the earth has become disconnected from the rest of the universe, and an extraterrestrial dimension of life surveys the earth. Certain earthlings—those who form this group, of course—have been chosen to be contacted by these extraterrestrials to help heal this cosmic rift! This is so far out I can hardly fathom mature adults believing it.

On a more serious note, behaviorism insists that people are basically good. Our hurtful behavior and the wrong choices we make are the result of the negative influences we have experienced. If we deal with the negative influences in society, people will behave differently and the world will be a better place to live.

This may sound very kind and comforting, but it's patently untrue. People are fallen. No amount of effort spent in removing negative influences and experiences will change the selfish human heart. Behaviorism is the wrong medicine for the problem of sin.

Quoting the prophet Isaiah, Jesus said of the religious leaders of his time, "'These people honor me with their lips, but their hearts are far from me. They worship me in vain; their teachings are but rules taught by men.'... Leave them; they are blind guides. If a blind man leads a blind man, both will fall into a pit" (Matthew 15:8,9,14, NIV). If we allow human reasoning, no matter how convincing it sounds, to guide us, we will be like the blind being led by the blind. It is the Word of God, not the ideas of people, that is to be our guide for how we live our lives.

The Bible Calls Selfishness Sin

Sin is the reason our world isn't getting better and better. Because of Adam, sin entered the world. Every subsequent person on this planet has ratified the original sin of Adam, and spiritual death has spread to all mankind *because everyone has sinned* (Romans 5:12). Though sin entered the world through one man, the entire human race is separated from God, and every individual must give an account for his selfish choices. Jeremiah 31:30 states, "But every one shall die for his own sin; each man who eats sour grapes, his teeth shall be set on edge."

When God judged Cain for slaying his brother Abel, He told him, "Why are you angry, and why has your countenance fallen? If you do well, will you not be accepted? And if you do not do well, sin is crouching at the door; its desire is for you, but you must master it" (Genesis 4:6,7). We must master sin. God will accept no excuses for its presence in our life. We cannot point the finger at others. Each person will stand before the judge of all the earth to give an account of his life. Only by facing our selfishness and accepting responsibility for it before God will we be able to receive His grace and mercy.

The law of God tells us what God is like—and what we are like. God's law reveals a need that only God's grace can supply. Only by honestly facing our own selfishness will we be able to find God's grace. God's Spirit is sent to convict us of our sin. As we acknowledge our guilt and responsibility, the Holy Spirit illumines our mind to understand the grace of God and what Jesus has done for us on the cross.

That's what I would have told the Bahai woman in the airport restaurant had our conversation continued. I would have told her she was wrong, that we are not on the brink of heralding a beautiful new world full of love and understanding. If we want a better world then we must strike at the root of the problem: the hearts and minds of men and women which, though noble in many of their pursuits, are tainted by sin. Government leaders today have affairs, dump their spouses, lie to the public, break campaign pledges, and seem devoid of personal integrity. What makes us think that leaders without moral backbone will be able to forge enduring links of peace, understanding, love, and unity which will usher in a beautiful new world? It can't happen until the problem of sin is solved in each individual's life.

Consider other evidences that our world is beseiged by the selfishness which rules the human heart. Crime is on the increase, and rape is the fastest growing crime in America. The average marriage lasts seven years. Fifty percent of the marriages in the United States break up within three years. An estimated 130,000 handguns are taken to high school every day.

One teenage boy expressed a more realistic view of America than the deluded followers of Bahaullah, though he was just as confused. He scribbled these words on a Los Angeles ghetto wall before he joined a satanic cult: "Ashes to ashes, dust to dust. If God won't help us, Satan must."

We are witnessing in America the emergence of a generation of moral misfits devoid of any sense of right or wrong. Many teens have no understanding of personal responsibility for their actions and show little remorse for sins against society. One boy coolly expressed his plan of vengeance against his father:

> My father used to beat my mom all the time. That makes me kind of angry. He was always out partying, getting high. My fantasy is making him suffer. First I'd shoot him in the kneecaps and let him suffer for about an hour, screaming. Then I'd shoot him ... [again] and let him suffer some more, and then I'd put a bullet through his head.[2]

These are not lines from some sick horror movie script. They are the words of a 17-year-old boy in a treatment program in San Bernardino, California, where he is being treated for sexually molesting younger members of his family. Nor is this an isolated case of disturbed teens in need of psychiatric care. It is reported that private psychiatric beds for teenagers is the fastest growing segment of the hospital industry.

As Christians we cannot offer platitudes about how much better the world is getting or how much more enlightened and sophisticated people are today. All we can offer is the truth: The problem in the world is selfishness in human hearts, and only Jesus Christ can truly change a selfish heart.

Each of us has within us the capacity to be unbelievably selfish. First John 1:8 instructs us, "If we say we have no sin, we deceive ourselves, and the truth is not in us." The writer of Proverbs laments, "Who can say, 'I have made my heart clean; I am pure from my sin'?" (Proverbs 20:9). Everyone has a sinful nature. That nature may not be as recognizable in some as it was in the man who beat his unborn child to death, but nonetheless it is there.

Jesus has some hard things to say about the selfishness of the human heart, things I doubt the Bahai woman in the restaurant would have wanted to hear. He said, "You have heard that it was said to the people long ago, 'Do not murder, and anyone who murders will be subject to judgment.' But I tell you that anyone who is angry with his brother will be subject to judgment.... You have heard that it was said, 'Do not commit adultery.' But I tell you that anyone who looks at a woman lustfully has already committed adultery with her in his heart" (Matthew 5:21,22,27,28, NIV).

Was Jesus trying to tell His disciples that every time they were angry they committed murder, or that every time they had lustful thoughts they committed adultery? Obviously not. When I'm angry with someone he doesn't drop dead at my feet. Jesus is saying that murder is the ultimate outworking of anger and that adultery is the ultimate outworking of lust, and that each one of us has the roots of these actions within us. Furthermore, the sins of the heart such as anger and lust are the same as sinful physical acts such as murder and adultery. One is no worse than the other, though we often judge people more harshly for their outward behavior. God sees the heart. The roots of these heinous outward sins are firmly embedded in everyone. Just because they are invisible doesn't mean they are not there.

Dealing with Selfishness at Its Source

What's the problem with our world? Sin. The title of this chapter asks another important question: Whose problem is it anyway? The biblical answer is simple but profound and sobering for every believer: Each one of us is responsible. Limiting sin's outworking in society is the responsibility of those who have been called to holiness. The spirit of the age has no platform in the world except what we allow it through our own selfish, sinful choices.

If we want to see people turn back toward biblical morality, we must not consider ourselves better than the society which surrounds us. Rather we must ask ourselves how deep the roots of sin we judge in others are in our own hearts. Do we cry for stiffer penalties for murderers while struggling with a problem with anger? Do we denounce the tide of immorality which is sweeping over our land while ogling pornographic movies or magazines when no one is looking? In order to deal with the sins which characterize the spirit of the age in our culture, we must first look into our own hearts and see what lurks there. We will never see our society change for the better until we deal with the sin in ourselves.

I firmly believe that the lack of holiness in the church in America is the cause of many of the sin problems in society. A holy church, separate from the world, is the salt which is necessary to preserve and flavor a godless society. When we blend into our culture instead of separating ourselves from its patterns through holy living, we have lost our "saltness." Jesus said, "You are the salt of the earth; but if salt has lost its taste, how shall its saltness be restored? It is no longer good for anything except to be thrown out and trodden under foot by men" (Matthew 5:13). To the extent that we Christians ignore Christ's call to holiness, to that extent the culture around us is captured by the spirit of the age.

This principle is illustrated in the life of Jonah. When God first called him to go declare His word to Nineveh, Jonah rebelled. He jumped on a ship going away from Nineveh. The storm which came up was the result of Jonah's disobedience. His disobedience also put the sailors on the ship in peril. Just as Jonah's rebellion brought the storm on the heathens sailing with him, so the church's lack of holiness in the world has caused the dam to break and a flood of unrighteousness to swamp the land.

The heathen on Jonah's ship had more integrity than Jonah. At least they called on their gods, and they were indignant that Jonah was disobeying his God. Many non-Christians today react the same way. They are repulsed by believers who ape the world around them. It is a sad day when secular journalists are used by God to point the finger of prophetic judgment at a worldly and hypocritical church.

I recently read the results of a survey that examined the differences between self-confessed "religious Christians" and "nonreligious non-Christians." The researchers concluded that religiosity is linked to less tolerance for popularly disliked groups such as heavy drinkers, those with a criminal record, left-wing extremists, and homosexuals. Because those being surveyed were professing Christians, and because Christians are supposed to represent Christ to the world, perhaps we should reword this conclusion to read: "Jesus is less tolerant than others of popularly disliked groups. He stays away from heavy drinkers, refuses to associate with criminals, scorns homosexuals, and has no sympathy whatsoever for those who want to change the system."

Is this the Jesus of the gospels? Is this the One who talked with Gentiles, ate with tax collectors, befriended the downtrodden, and culminated His life dying on a cross between two common thieves? No, the Jesus of the Bible hated sin—and He clearly separated Himself from it—but He loved sinners and ministered to them. Tragically, the church today is seen in a completely different light. *We have the reputation of enjoying sin while hating sinners.*

The first step to solving the problem of sin in the world is recognizing that selfishness in the lives of believers is the number one problem in society. Society doesn't need more social programs, more special interest groups, more money, more material goods, or more technology to solve its sin problem. Nor does it need another mass movement of placard-carrying Christians with maximum media coverage calling for others to repent of *their* wrongdoing. What our nation needs to see is changed Christians—believers who are not too proud to look into their hearts and deal with the selfishness they find lurking there.

Though we grow frustrated with an increasingly immoral society, the focus of our efforts for change should be the church. Imagine the impact on our society if all the Americans who call themselves born-again Christians— that's one-third of the entire population!—truly and unhypocritically lived out their faith after the manner of Jesus. If that kind of change took place in us, there would be an instant and unstoppable change in our nation.

Many of us throw up our hands and say, "Pipe dream; it'll never happen. It's just too hard to live that kind of a Christian life in today's world." Pipe dream? It may be for some, but it doesn't have to be so. It is possible to live a life of uncompromised obedience to Christ in today's world, but only if we stop aping the wealthy trendsetters who think heaven couldn't be better than life on Wall Street.

—4—
Heaven Couldn't Be Better Than This

M ultimillionaire Malcolm Forbes lived the good life. He owned castles and yachts, ran with bikers and movie stars, and tried desperately to prove his maxim of life, "He who has the most toys wins."

Malcolm Forbes had many toys. At the time of his death, estimates of Forbes' wealth ranged from $400 million to $1.25 billion. He owned eight homes which included a 40-acre estate in New Jersey, a palace in Tangier, Morocco, a chateau in Normandy, and an island in Fiji. Forbes also had accumulated 2,200 paintings and 12 Russian Imperial Faberge eggs, more than even the Soviet government possesses.

Forbes flaunted his wealth. He entertained royalty on his 151-foot, helicopter-equipped yacht, the *Highlander*. He jetted around the world in his private Boeing 727 named the *Capitalist Tool*. In August 1989 his $2 million seventieth birthday bash in Morocco sparked acrimonious debate in the media about the morality of such conspicuous consumption. Yet Forbes saw himself as the embodiment of the limitless success possible only in America. He directed that his ashes be buried under a marker with the epitaph, "While alive, he lived."

His funeral reflected the contrasts which marked his flamboyant life. As mourners gathered in the hushed sanctuary of prestigious St. Bartholomew's Episcopal Church in New York City, the haunting cry of a lone bagpipe gave way to the roar of motorcycle engines outside. In their own salute to Malcolm Forbes, about three dozen leather-swathed bikers gunned their Harleys during an impromptu procession up Park Avenue. The roaring engines elicited little surprise from Forbes's rich and famous friends inside the church. They knew the contrast only typified the multimillionaire's roller-coaster existence from the heights of big-business hobnobbing to swift plunges into the dark side of pleasure, to rumors of homosexuality.

Shortly before his death Forbes was interviewed on a television program. He said, "All I want to do is live long enough to enjoy all that I have." A participant from the audience asked Forbes if he believed in life after death. He answered, "Life after death will be no comparison to the life I am now living. I have the best possible life right now. It could never be any better."

Heaven couldn't be better than this? In a world of wars, poverty, homelessness, and drugs, heaven couldn't be better than this? While hundreds of thousands are being killed in senseless wars in the Middle East and millions are dying in North African famines, heaven couldn't be better than this?

Caught Up in the American Dream

Malcolm Forbes epitomized our society's search for self-fulfillment and the good life. Popular literature is consumed with the joys and pleasures of self, exaggerating the values of fame, success, materialism, and comfort. But time has shown that each new glittering promise of self-fulfillment leads only to self-absorption, isolation, and addiction to self-gratification. The fruits of these selfish pursuits are introspection, insecurity, loneliness, and a lifestyle that defines fulfillment as the act of looking for the meaning of life.

Decades of seemingly limitless affluence in the United States have succeeded only in sucking our culture dry of character, leaving us spiritually empty and economically self-absorbed. Our nation is filled with frightened, hollow people. If heaven isn't any better than this, we're in trouble.

Rather than standing apart from this futile search for prosperity and the good life, Christians have been caught up in it. We have absorbed the same value system as our troubled culture. We have our own celebrities, our own success gospel, and our own sermons on prosperity, wealth, and health.

We are preoccupied with the same values that have prevented the message of the gospel from changing society. We have aborted our role as the church in America. To Christians immersed in the American dream, victory means success, discipleship means getting what you can out of life, overcoming means avoiding, freedom means self-will, happiness means pleasure, and fullness of life means accumulating more and more possessions.

When we absorb the values of the culture which surrounds us, how can we be separate from it? Holiness does not call us to get more *out* of life, but to put more of ourselves *into* life. Holiness means that we are set free from the cycle of inwardness and self-awareness and set apart from the world. Holiness means that we can live a life that resists the spirit of the age. Holiness sets the Christian free to live above the fads of fulfillment and seek the Person who personifies life itself. John 17:3 says, "And this is eternal life, that they know thee the only true God, and Jesus Christ whom thou hast sent."

Counterfeit Christianity

The Bible speaks of two roads: the narrow road which leads to life and the broad road which leads to destruction (Matthew 7:13,14). But many American preachers today are proclaiming a middle road to heaven, a counterfeit Christianity: the gospel of the good life. They preach a gospel of salvation without submission, discipleship without discipline, conversion without confession of sin, love without law, and reformation without repentance. Counterfeit Christianity teaches that people can receive Jesus as Savior without receiving Him as Lord, and be followers of Christ while still serving themselves. This phony gospel embraces a brand of grace that is a disgrace. It is a religion of carnality, and we must turn away from it.

Many preachers and Christian workers are stumped as to why there are so many sinning Christians these days. But it is no wonder when Christians have absorbed the values of the nation in which we live. The gospel preached on the airwaves is a gospel of prosperity and self-advancement. Counterfeit Christianity promises a guaranteed ticket to heaven with discipleship being only optional. Counterfeit Christians can be moral, outwardly prayerful, zealous in good works, conscientious, generous, and well respected by others while being devoid of the faith that will grant them eternal life. Counterfeit Christians can glorify God, give money, believe in Christ, go to church, and pray—all for the wrong reasons. If we take the Bible seriously, we see that a person ultimately cannot live for himself and still be a Christian. Yet many are teaching this doctrine. If we are to rise above the spirit of the age we must call people to complete commitment to Christ.

In Galatians 5:16-26 Paul compares the person who

walks in the flesh to the person who walks in the Spirit. He says the fleshly person participates freely in "immorality, impurity, licentiousness, idolatry, sorcery, enmity, strife, jealousy, anger, selfishness, dissension, party spirit, envy, drunkenness, carousing, and the like" (vv. 19-21). But the person who walks in the Spirit bears the fruit of "love, joy, peace, patience, kindness, goodness, faithfulness, gentleness, and self-control" (vv. 22,23). A carnal person's life is dominated by the deeds of the flesh with only occasional glimmers of the fruit of the Spirit. This is not true Christianity; it's counterfeit. It's the kind of Christianity which results when the good-life gospel is preached and believed. In contrast, a Christian who walks in the Spirit may at times commit carnal acts, but he does not live by the desires of the flesh as a matter of practice.

Revive Us Again

The history of Christianity reveals that we often turn God's dealings with people into spiritual movements which eventually degenerate into cold, religious machinery. Church leaders spend more time maintaining and managing the system than seeking God. Though all great evangelical movements start with spiritual life, they seem to get caught in a downward spiral which leads to legalism, materialism, liberalism, and eventually idolatry. Christians must experience periodic times of revival and renewal of holiness or they will lose their power to impact society.

The church in America desperately needs revival today. It is time to "break up your fallow ground, for it is the time to seek the Lord, that he may come and rain salvation upon you" (Hosea 10:12). The American church has suffered the same collapse of character that is so widespread in our culture. Christians today are characterized by a lack of radical obedience. Our leaders are afraid of calling us to true holiness for fear we will stop attending church or stop giving. C.S. Lewis aptly described fallow-hearted American Christians when he wrote, "A world of nice people, content in their own niceness, looking no further, turned away from God, would be just as desperately in need of salvation as a miserable world—and might even be more difficult to save."[1]

Many years ago Sally and I traveled across the United States in a beat-up Volkswagen van. We had only been married a few months, and the organization we work with, Youth With A Mission (YWAM), was in its early days. We had been asked by YWAM's founder Loren Cunningham to pick up a van load of dried soup mix, which had been donated to YWAM by the Campbell soup company in New Jersey, and to deliver it to California. We filled the van with cartons and traveled across the states living on soup and Christian hospitality!

I had heard that Arizona highway patrolmen were tough on speeders, so when we crossed into Arizona I was very careful to stay within the speed limit. But late one night while driving across a lonely stretch of desert, I saw the dreaded flashing red lights in my rearview mirror. I pulled to the side of the road and the patrolman approached the driver's window.

"Let me see your driver's license," he growled. I dutifully complied. After studying my license carefully he asked me to get out of the van and follow him back to his patrol car. I did as he asked, leaving a praying wife in the front seat of the van. "Get in," he said, "I need to talk with you." I couldn't imagine what was wrong.

As I settled into the front seat of the patrol car the officer looked me in the eye and said, "I'm going to have to write up a ticket."

"A ticket?" I exclaimed. "Was I driving over the speed limit? I thought I was just driving 65 miles per hour."

"That's correct, young man," the officer replied. "But I'm going to have to give you a warning ticket. You were almost speeding."

Almost speeding? I thought. I'd never heard of a warning ticket for almost speeding.

As the officer wrote up the warning ticket he began telling me about his Christian faith, which I thought was unusual since I had said nothing about being a Christian or working with YWAM. The ticket-writing process took longer and longer as the officer became more detailed in his explanation of what it meant for a person to put faith in Christ.

It suddenly dawned on me that this man had pulled me over under the guise of giving me a warning ticket in order to share his Christian faith with me. I'd never been witnessed to by a policeman-evangelist before, so I decided to play along with him. I asked all the right questions: What does it mean to be a Christian? What do I have to do to be saved? And he gave me all the right answers.

After a while I decided to come clean. "You'll be happy to know, sir," I interjected, "that I love Jesus too. I'm a born-again Christian. I accepted Him as my personal Savior when I was nine years old. I work full-time with a Christian organization."

The officer looked me in the eye again thoughtfully, then reached into the backseat of the patrol car and pulled out a huge family Bible. He thumbed through it, ran his fingers down a page, pointed at a verse, and said, "The Bible says that many will call Him Lord, but fail to do what He says. Young man, it's not enough to profess to be a Christian. You have to make Jesus the Lord of your life!"

I could hardly believe my ears. This man was not satisfied with my confession of Christ as Savior. He wanted to make sure that I possessed Him fully and completely as Lord! After I convinced him that Jesus was the Lord of my life, we had a great time of prayer together, and I joyfully informed my anxiously waiting wife that all was well.

Overcoming the spirit of the age does not happen simply when people confess Christ as Lord. Jesus said it is possible to call Him Lord and fail to do what He tells us to do (Luke 6:46). Holy Christians not only want church buildings filled with people but holy people filled with God. A move of God in our nation will not only result in a greater number of professions of Christianity, it also will profoundly impact the way people live. True revivals result in changed lives. And America desperately needs to look at Christians and see changed lives.

A Change of Direction

The revival of holiness that American Christianity so desperately needs will begin with both individual and corporate repentance. This is the only way we can continually overcome the spirit of the age. Repentance literally means to turn around and head in the opposite direction. It describes a change of mind that leads to a change of life. John the Baptist proclaimed repentance in the wilderness (Matthew 3:2). Jesus began His public ministry challenging His followers to repent (Mark 1:14,15). Peter called for repentance on the day of Pentecost (Acts 3:19). Paul preached repentance from house to house (Acts 17:30). And God still demands it from us today.

Repentance Means Obedience

Everywhere Jesus went He proclaimed the twofold message of repentance and faith in God (Mark 1:15). The faith He proclaimed was not mere mental assent, but the kind of faith that produces change in people's lives. There is no such thing as biblical faith that does not produce obedience. In fact, it's impossible to separate believing in God from obeying God. Romans 1:5 tells us that Paul called people to the "obedience of faith." Revival will only come when Christians turn from a hollow confession of faith to an active obedience of faith.

It is important to note that the Bible identifies both a true and a false repentance. Second Corinthians 7:10 says, "Godly grief produces a repentance that leads to salvation and brings no regret, but worldly grief produces death." Godly grief is true repentance, and true repentance is more than contrition. A person may be sorrowful over his sins yet unrepentant because he is sorrowing for the wrong reasons. Instead of sorrowing because his sins have hurt and disappointed God, he may just feel bad because his sins have been personally painful, stressful, or costly, or because his sins have been found out. If there is no change in character, there has been no true repentance.

True repentance is also more than confession. Just as someone can visit a psychologist and feel relieved after unloading the burden of guilt from wrong choices, so a person can feel emotionally relieved by confessing his sins to God. This relief of the emotional burden of guilt, called catharsis, is not the same as biblical confession of sin. To acknowledge our sin to God means that we are ready to abandon that sin and turn to God for forgiveness. To confess our sins to God in the biblical sense is to accept responsibility for our sins, being fully prepared to do whatever God asks of us to rid ourselves of them.

True repentance is also more than conviction of sin. Charles Finney, the great American revivalist, found that there were various attitudes toward sin and repentance. Finney spoke about careless sinners, awakened sinners, convicted sinners, and sinners who are anxious to change their lives.

I once spoke to a careless sinner in Jamaica who said to me, "I understand the gospel, but I'm not willing to obey it. I'm living for myself. I know that I deserve hell, and when I die I will go there. But I don't care." Careless sinners have no interest in repentance.

I think we all recognize people who are awakened to God's holiness and their own unrighteousness, and are disturbed by what they see. But this awakening is often followed by an attitude of anger or self-justification. Just because a person is awakened to his sad spiritual state does not mean he has repented of his sins.

The convicted sinner is convinced he has sinned and knows he needs God, but he is unwilling to change. Knowing that you are a rebel against God and that you deserve punishment is still not the same as turning from your sins. True repentance happens when the Holy Spirit illumines our heart and makes us aware that we are wrong, and we respond by turning to God, crying out for mercy and changing our sinful behavior.

The results of false repentance are seen everywhere in the church. Hearts are unbroken. Sin is covered up. Changes in character are only partial or temporary. Self-righteousness abounds. Consciences are seared. Believers are disobedient. And many professing Christians do not walk in the light with God and one another. The fruit of true repentance is a change of mind, heart, and behavior. The truly repentant person not only admits the guilt of his sin, but takes responsibility for what he has done against God.

Repentance Means Seeing God's Point of View

True repentance is the result of seeing our selfishness from God's point of view through the illumination of the Holy Spirit. I'll never forget as a young boy being awakened by loud banging on the door of our home, the church parsonage, at three o'clock one morning. My father opened the door to find Clifford Mullins, the young man who led our church youth group, weeping and crying out for help.

Clifford had been at home fasting and praying, seeking more of God, longing to be free from sins that had dominated his life. As he sought God alone, Clifford had received a clear picture from God about the ugly sin in his heart. He had come to my father broken and repentant.

My father prayed with him for the assurance of forgiveness from his sins, and Clifford left our home a changed man. As a result of Clifford's repentance, revival ignited our little congregation. Scores of people came to the Lord, and many went into full-time Christian service—all because one man dared to see his heart as God sees it.

Repentance Means Making Things Right

Repentance also means restitution. Matthew 5:23,24 teaches that a truly repentant person is willing to rectify any misdeeds he has committed against others. Restitution means repairing the damage our sin has caused. It means returning the property we have stolen from work, from the store, or from a friend. It means going to the person we have offended or slandered and asking their forgiveness. It means repairing the damage our sin has caused as much as is humanly possible. We don't effect restitution in order to be saved, but *because* we are saved.

Repentance Is an Ongoing Process

Repentance is not a onetime event. It is a process by which Christians individually and the church corporately live in holiness. It is an attitude of life. It is the day-by-day process of living under the lordship of Christ. We see the awesome holiness of God and the horrible consequences of sin, and we respond with heartfelt contrition, confession, and change of character.

The following questions will help you assess the spiritual state of your heart. They will help you discern the influence of the spirit of the age in your life. I encourage you to work through them prayerfully and allow God to speak to you. They are not meant to condemn you but to guide you in devoting your life to Jesus. Your answers will reveal your willingness to be separate from the spirit of the age and your preparedness to live a holy life.

1. *Am I growing spiritually?* Am I facing my spiritual condition honestly? Is my relationship with the Lord alive and growing? Do I desire to be with the Lord in prayer and Bible study? Am I dealing with sin quickly, confessing it to God and others?

2. *Is God in control?* Is there anything in my life that challenges God's supremacy as absolute ruler and Lord over all I do? Is there any area of my life that I am consciously holding back from the Lord? Am I willing to do anything anywhere at any time He would ask of me? Is he Lord of my family life? free time? relationships?

3. *Do I get my spiritual food from God and His Word?* Recognizing that I cannot grow spiritually without prayer and Bible study, am I being nourished regularly by meaningful study in God's Word and time spent in prayer alone and with other believers?

4. *Is sin hindering God's blessing in my life?* Have I covered over any sins trying to forget them or hide them from myself, God, or others? Have I failed to ask forgiveness for my part in any relationships, past or present, which have gone wrong?

5. *Am I accountable to other Christians?* Am I part of a meaningful fellowship of believers who are accountable to God and one another? Do I share with them my fears, sins, and joys? Do they know me well and hold me accountable by asking hard questions about my thought life, my devotional life, my relationships with my family and friends, and my financial obligations?

6. *Am I sharing my faith with non-Christians on a regular basis?* Do I know and pray for many non-Christians by name? Am I concerned enough for them to get meaningfully involved in their lives? Are people coming to know Christ because of my witness? How long has it been since I personally led someone to Christ?

7. *Do I seek God's will and direction in every major decision in life?* Do I listen to His voice? Do I pray expectantly, really believing that He will speak to me and answer me? Am I so close to God and on such intimate terms with Him that He can speak to me anytime He wishes?

8. *Do I know Jesus better than any of my earthly friends?* Do I turn to Him before anyone else when I am in need? Am I becoming like Him because of our friendship? Can I honestly say that my values, priorities, and character reflect the nature and character of Jesus?

9. *Am I caught up in the spirit of the age?* Am I materialistic or independent? Have I pushed God to the margins of my life? Am I so overwhelmed with modern life that I have withdrawn from others? Do I think God owes me a good life: health, wealth, happiness, etc.? Am I actively pursuing these things?

10. *Do I fear the Lord?* Am I more concerned with what people think of me than with what the Lord thinks of me? Am I more concerned with my reputation than with God's reputation? Do I hate sin? Is my friendship with the Lord the most important thing in my life?

I wish I could have shared the gospel with Malcolm Forbes. I hope that someone reached him because now it is too late. But it is not too late for you and me. We have the opportunity to live for Christ. Heaven is better than this life, and heaven begins now by knowing and obeying the Lord Jesus. He is our hope. He is our reason to live a holy life.

— 5 —
Why Holiness?

I n the next 30 minutes in America 29 teenagers will attempt suicide, 22 girls will have abortions, 685 teens will use some form of drugs, and 228 kids will be physically or sexually abused by their parents. Is there any doubt that we need the influence of holiness in our nation?

A federal judge recently struck down as unconstitutional parts of a child pornography law that would have required porn publishers to document the ages of their models. He said that the record-keeping requirements of the law *overburdened the producers of pornographic material*! Is there any doubt that we need the influence of holiness in our nation?

In a survey of more than 200,000 freshmen entering 90 colleges, 76 percent listed financial prosperity as an essential or very important goal for life, and 71 percent said that making money was their chief reason for going to college. We need a revival in America today, a revival of biblical holiness. Is there *any* doubt that we need the influence of holiness in our nation?

In the previous four chapters we determined that Christians today live in a society which is unsympathetic and often hostile to the lifestyle of holiness to which we have been called in Jesus Christ. We are like birds in a cage, surrounded by a culture in the throes of a crisis of character induced by Satan and the cultural forces which constitute the spirit of the age. And at the heart of the crisis is the sin which rules in the heart of every unbelieving man and woman in our nation.

We also acknowledged that the people of God in America have largely failed to separate themselves from the spirit of the age. Rather, many have compromised themselves to the spirit of the age by adopting a comfortable counterfeit Christianity in which they enjoy Jesus as Savior but fail to obey Him as Lord. Instead of influencing their culture, they have been seduced by it. As their culture continues to close in around them, they stand in desperate need of repentance, revival, and renewal.

Some of us may be tempted to think, "What's the use? Why fight it? Why work so hard to be holy in such a hopelessly unholy culture?" As we have noted, some of the teaching in the body of Christ today suggests that holiness is an option, and not a requirement, for the believer. Yet Hebrews 12:14 clearly declares, "Make every effort to live in peace with all men and to be holy; without holiness no one will see the Lord" (NIV). Before we explore the influential nature of the spirit of the age in Part Two of this book, we must understand the *why* of holiness.

A Positive Response to What God Has Done

We can't really comprehend what God is asking us to do in Hebrews 12:14 without first realizing what He has done for us, as summarized earlier in Hebrews: "We have been made holy through the sacrifice of the body of Jesus

Christ once for all" (10:10, NIV). God is calling us to a life of practical holiness in the world in response to what He has already done for us on the cross. Put another way, in response to the salvation God has provided, He beckons us to "work out your own salvation with fear and trembling; for God is at work in you, both to will and to work for his good pleasure" (Philippians 2:12,13).

Three truths from Scripture emphasize why a life of holiness is the only acceptable response to what God has done for us. First, Ephesians 2:8 states that salvation "is the gift of God." God offers to save us from sin and set us free from the spirit of the age. We are saved by God's grace through faith. It is not something we have earned through good deeds. We can't take credit for it in any way. We are totally indebted to Jesus for our salvation. Such indebtedness demands a love response to Jesus. *A life of holy, obedient service to God shows that we are grateful for what God has done.*

Second, Ephesians 2:10 reveals that we are saved by the Lord Jesus "for good works, which God prepared beforehand, that we should walk in them." God has redeemed us not only from our past sin but to live a holy life now. Our response of holy living was part of God's design in saving us. It is His plan for our lives. It shows that we are being conformed to His character.

Finally, Christ died not only to take the punishment for our sin but also to deliver us from the misery of our sin. He died in our stead so that we could be empowered by the Holy Spirit to live a holy life.

When we trust in Christ for the forgiveness of our sins the Holy Spirit comes and dwells within us. He cleanses us and washes us from the impurities of sin. He transforms our inner nature so that we are conformed to the likeness of Christ. First Peter 3:18 says, "For Christ died for your sins once for all, the righteous for the unrighteous, to bring you to God." We are able to enter into the presence of God because of Christ's death for us. He has transformed us and empowered us. Without the indwelling Holy Spirit we would not have the power to conquer sin. Through God's gift of salvation, the resurrected Christ comes to live in us. He is all-powerful, and He makes His power available to us to conquer sin.

There are times when I have not felt like a powerful Christian. When I sin or disobey God, I feel guilty, confused, and defeated. Even though God did not intend for us to live that way, He understands when we fail. But He does not intend for us to grovel in our misery. We must face up to our failure, confess it to God, and ask His forgiveness. If we accept responsibility for our sin and ask God to show us His grief over sin, then we can experience the joy of fresh forgiveness. This is also part of God's wonderful gift of salvation.

A Solemn Warning to Be Heeded

What does the writer of Hebrews mean when he says, "Without holiness no one will see the Lord" (12:14 NIV)? He is warning believers to take seriously God's command to live holy, obedient lives. Our daily expression of holiness is a reflection of our faith in Christ. If we have no desire to be holy, we should seriously question the genuineness of our faith in the Lord Jesus.

Christ not only died to save us from the punishment for our sins, but also from slavery to sin in this worldly culture. To continue to live in sin as a Christian is contradictory to the most basic meaning of Christianity. Christ died to save us *from* our sins, not to let us remain *in* our sins (Matthew 1:21; 1 John 1:6,7). What kind of person would want to follow Christ and not desire to live a holy life? If so-called Christians are not consecrated to God, then we can doubt whether they are truly converted by God. Based on the teaching of Scripture, we would have to question their sincerity and salvation.

Holiness, then, is not an option for the believer. Paul wrote to Titus, "For the grace of God has appeared for the salvation of all men, training us to renounce irreligion and worldly passions, and to live sober, upright, and godly lives in this world" (Titus 2:11,12). Though holiness is not a condition for salvation, it is the natural consequence of salvation. We do not become holy in order to be saved, but because we are saved. We do not do good works to get to heaven, but because heaven has already come into our hearts.

To trust Christ for salvation is to trust him for holiness. If there is no desire for holiness within, then it is doubtful that the Holy Spirit has come to dwell within. The Holy Spirit does not save us without giving us the desire to live a holy life.

Reasons for Holiness

There are three reasons why holiness is not optional for the believer.

First, holiness is required because it enables us to have *fellowship with God*. First John 1:6 states, "If we say that we have fellowship with Him, and walk in darkness, we lie and do not practice the truth" (NKJV).

Second, holiness is required for *our own well-being*. God gave His laws governing our behavior for our good. When we obey God's laws, we are living in a manner consistent with God's intended purpose for us. When we disobey, we pay a price. Just as an automobile engine would be destroyed if you poured Coca-Cola into the gas tank instead of gasoline, so we suffer when we break God's laws: guilt, fear, confusion, physical sickness, relationship breakdowns, and many other physical, emotional, and spiritual consequences. David lamented the physical consequences from his sin: "When I declared not my sin, my body wasted away through my groaning all the day long"

(Psalm 32:3). Sin destroys us, but holiness brings peace of mind.

The Bible says, "He who sows to his own flesh will from the flesh reap corruption" (Galatians 6:8). Sin has consequences. When we break God's law, God's law breaks us. It's the exact opposite of how God intended for us to live. But even the consequences of our sin are an evidence of God's love. The New Testament says, "The Lord disciplines those he loves, and he punishes everyone he accepts as a son" (Hebrews 12:6, NIV).

The third reason for holy living is that it is necessary for the *assurance of our salvation*. Salvation is by faith alone, but faith will always manifest itself in the good fruit of holiness. A Christian is a brand-new creation, and that will be evident in his life. A life of holiness and obedience on the outside is the encouraging fruit of a life of faith on the inside.

Heaven is for the holy. It is absurd to think that those who are unholy will even want to be in heaven. Revelation 22:11-14 reads, "He who is unjust, let him be unjust still; he who is filthy, let him be filthy still; he who is righteous, let him be righteous still; he who is holy, let him be holy still. And behold, I am coming quickly, and My reward is with Me, to give to every one according to his work. I am the Alpha and the Omega, the Beginning and the End, the First and the Last. Blessed are those who do His commandments, that they may have the right to the tree of life, and may enter through the gates into the city" (NKJV).

This is the holiness acceptable to God. This is the holiness necessary to repulse the spirit of the age.

PART 2

DISCERNING THE SPIRIT OF THE AGE

— 6 —
Satan's Servant Spirits

I remember speaking to a group of university students in New Zealand in 1977. During the question and answer period, one student asked me about my beliefs about the devil and spiritual warfare. I said, "Satan loves sin, fear, and attention, and I will not give him any of the three. Next question, please." I thought that by refusing to give time even to discuss the matter I was treating the question in an appropriate manner.

Later that evening as I sat alone reflecting on the day's events, I experienced deep sorrow. I didn't understand what I'd done wrong, but I felt I had somehow grieved the Holy Spirit in the course of the day. I prayed and asked the Lord what was wrong. My abrupt answer to the question about Satan suddenly came to mind, and I heard the Lord's voice inside me say, "I'm disappointed in your response. You have little knowledge of the spiritual realm and no discernment or authority over spiritual forces as my disciples had many years ago. Your answer reflects your own fears."

The words the Lord spoke to me that night pierced my soul. I had no authority in the area of evil spiritual forces. What had been elementary to the discipleship training of the early Christians was missing in my life. Instead, my response to the subject was fear well-disguised in theological terms. It may have fooled some, but it did not fool the Lord. I was afraid of the unknown. I was afraid of extremism. I was afraid of the devil. I was greatly bothered by the fact people were in spiritual need, but I could not help anyone because of my spiritual impotence. It alarmed me that I could be manipulated by demonic spirits because of my lack of discernment and power.

That night in New Zealand I read the words of Jesus from Matthew 10:1: "And he called to him his twelve disciples and gave them authority over unclean spirits." I asked the Lord to teach me about spiritual powers at work in our world. And I asked Him for discernment and spiritual authority over unclean spirits. I prayed a simple prayer asking God to take away my fear and to give me the authority He gave to His disciples many years ago.

Nothing dramatic or emotional happened that night, but my prayer put me in a frame of mind to learn. I began to study God's Word to find out about spiritual powers. My study launched me into a spiritual odyssey of learning about Satan and his principalities.

Satan Is Alive and Well

In the process of studying the Scriptures I learned Satan is the prince of the power of the air and that he is at work in those who are disobedient (Ephesians 2:2). The apostle Paul told Timothy about a coming apostasy, warning that some men would be captured by Satan to do his will (2 Timothy 2:26). He told the Corinthians, "The god of this age has blinded the minds of the unbelievers" (2 Corinthians 4:4). I learned that Satan attacks our mind (2 Corinthians 10:4,5), our character (Ephesians 2:1,2), our faith in God (Ephesians 6:16), our theology (2 Corinthians 11:14), and our family (Job 1–42).

I began to take seriously that Satan is the god of this age, and that we are subject to his wiles as he seeks to dominate and rule the culture in which we live. Satan blinds nonbelievers, prompts disobedience, captures people to do his will, and rules the spiritual atmosphere around us. I realized that we must be alert to his attempts to subvert our faith and compromise our walk with God. If Peter was subject to the thoughts of Satan (Matthew 16:23), we can be as well.

Living in a fallen world requires us to accept spiritual warfare as part of our daily existence. We confront evil in every corner of life. Spiritual forces have captured American culture. It is the greatest of all follies to ignore the battle or treat it lightly. Whether out of ignorance, fear, or both, many believers try to "leave well enough alone," thinking—as I did—that if they ignore Satan and his wiles he will not affect them personally. But Satan is the god of this present evil age, and we must discern his spiritual attacks on us. If we don't recognize Satan's work we cannot be holy people.

When we observe the superficial nature of American culture and its bent toward self-realization, leisure, compulsive spending, political passivity, and moral permissiveness, we must at least suspect the role of the demonic in the decline of Christian influence in our nation. Around the turn of the century a fundamental cultural transformation occurred in the United States. Prior to this time Western culture was oriented to the importance of work, savings, Christian morality, the nuclear family, and self-denial. Liberal Protestantism, the death of moral absolutes, and the acceptability and national marketing of self-indulgence all coalesced to open the door for the capture of our culture by spiritual principalities bent on turning us into a nation committed to the good life. As a result our culture is fixated on materialism and pleasure.

The erosion of Christian morality in every sphere of life is not just the result of the denial of biblical absolutes and other non-Christian cultural forces. Spiritual powers are always at work when evil is present. When men are disobedient and follow the passions of the flesh, their state is attributed to Satan's influence. We must consider the social problems of our nation within the context of spiritual opposition. We face large-scale problems of poverty, unemployment, prostitution, loneliness, chemical dependency, gang violence, abandoned and abused children, homelessness, and AIDS. Behind these symptoms we must see Satan trying to destroy our nation. If we ignore or downplay his role in the destruction of people and American society, we are missing what God's Word teaches us.

We must recognize the spiritual powers that have taken control of our nation. We are in enemy territory. The Bible says, "We are not contending against flesh and blood, but against the principalities, against the powers, against the world rulers of this present darkness, against the spiritual hosts of wickedness in the heavenly places" (Ephesians 6:12). God's Word is clear: Demonic powers are at work in the world. While we can easily envisage spiritism and the occult in non-Western nations, we have yet to take spiritual warfare at home seriously. Our battle for spiritual survival is all the more dangerous because Satan's tactics for the Western world are different than in places where spiritism and the occult are blatantly overt. In our culture, Satan has subtly and covertly infiltrated the good life and the American dream, and he beckons us to submerge ourselves in them.

Spiritual Powers in High Places

The "principalities" and "world rulers of this present darkness" (Ephesians 6:12) have gained control of the values, ideals, and character of our nation. We are no longer a nation under God. The New Testament Greek words for principalities and world rulers refer to spirit beings that have been given control of various parts of the cosmos. These terms suggest a hierarchy of beings in the demonic realm who have been assigned to specific places and tasks.

I believe Satan has assigned spiritual principalities and world rulers of darkness to America. These spiritual forces are evil, but they often go unrecognized because they encourage excesses in areas which are socially acceptable. For example, while principalities squeeze the life out of other countries through poverty, those responsible for America gorge us with prosperity. While other nations are steeped in ignorance, we are tempted to trust in education and technology instead of God. Satan's servant spirits in America are easy to overlook because they trade in such ostensibly "nice" goods. Their dominion over our land has resulted in a way of life that is appealing and comfortable, but ultimately destructive. Those who succeed in attaining the good life tend to trust in their wealth and success instead of God. And the greed which guides the good life withholds from others the time, energy, and resources needed to solve problems like poverty, homelessness, AIDS, and loneliness.

The following chapters look at several of these servant spirits, the principalities and powers which have taken control of American culture. It is vital that American believers understand these spirits and how they have influenced our nation. If we fail to understand evil and its grip on our culture we will expose ourselves as Christians to a subtle and insidious evil. The church in America today is caught up in the spirit of the age and is in danger of betraying the Lord Jesus for the good-life gospel. We may end up being unholy simply because we fail to perceive how Satan has captured the culture we are called to liberate.

— 7 —

The Good-Life Gospel!

One of the servant spirits of the age is epitomized by a Christian television personality I heard recently. "God wants to make you happy," he said. "He wants to fill your life with good things. He wants it to be more exciting than ever. He wants to make your business grow. Will you accept what Jesus can offer you? Will you come to Him and be blessed? It's your right to be blessed. Take what is yours. What have you got to lose? There is nothing to lose and everything to gain." The televangelist leaped about the stage as he spoke these words. His physical gyrations underscored his insistence that God is duty-bound to bless us and that it's our right to be blessed.

The same enthusiastic invitation to claim the health, wealth, and prosperity that "belongs" to us is being preached from many pulpits and espoused in many popular books today. I call it the good-life gospel, and it fits right in with the spirit of the age.

But is the good-life gospel really the message of Christ? Is God's primary goal that we be happy, healthy,

wealthy, and successful? Don't get me wrong: I believe that
God is the source of all the happiness we enjoy. And I
believe He is pleased to bless us. But His primary goal for
us is not temporal and material; it's spiritual and eternal.
Romans 14:17 reads, "For the Kingdom of God is not food
and drink, but righteousness and peace and joy in the Holy
Spirit" (NKJV). The blessings we receive in this life are the
by-products of fulfilling God's primary goal for us: serving
Him and others in the righteousness, peace, and joy of His
Spirit.

The good-life gospel is a very subtle and convincing
expression of the spirit of the age. It has seduced thousands
of believers. In a world sold out to self-fulfillment, Christians have been duped into believing that the good life is
their inheritance. Instead of calling us to lives of holiness
and service in a self-centered culture, the perpetrators of
the good-life gospel are urging us to grab what belongs to
us by divine right.

Let's examine more carefully the tenets of the good-
life gospel.

"God Wants to Make You Happy"

Isn't happiness what we all want for ourselves and our
families? But like so many other aspects of the Christian
life, happiness is a paradox. If we spend our lives trying to
attain it, we miss it. Happiness is the result of a life of
holiness, righteousness, and faithfulness to Jesus. If your
goal in life is to achieve happiness, you probably won't
reach your goal. But if your goal is to live a life dedicated to
God, happiness will be the by-product.

All around, we see people trying to produce their own
happiness. People spend thousands of dollars accumulating the latest gadgets, cruising the Caribbean, and spoiling
themselves at health clubs. But it seems that the more
they try to pamper themselves, the more they experience
emptiness. Trying to find meaning in a life lived solely for

personal happiness will destroy a person. No matter how much people pamper themselves, they cannot produce true happiness.

The idea that Jesus wants to lavish happiness on us apart from our commitment to a life of holiness and sacrificial service to others is just another disguise of the spirit of the age. The world says, "Live it up, spend, consume, enjoy. Be happy." The good-life gospel changes the formula only slightly: "Live it up, spend, consume, enjoy. God wants you happy." The same spirit of the age motivates both believers and nonbelievers; only the surface rationale is different. Christianity has merely translated the world's line into Christian lingo.

Countless numbers of believers are driven by the desire to consume to excess, to live for themselves, and to have a good time—a lifestyle which is incompatible with biblical holiness. The fact that so many believers have bought into the good-life gospel is an indication of how pervasive Satan's influence has become in the church.

The good-life gospel, which reaches out to believers with a promise of happiness, appeals to human selfishness instead of confronting the pain and perversity in which most Americans are trapped. The way out of the bondage to sin is the cross. Nothing can replace the truth that we must die to live. Jesus said, "If any man would come after me, let him deny himself and take up his cross and follow me. For whoever would save his life will lose it; and whoever loses his life for my sake and the gospel's will save it" (Mark 8:34,35).

Self-denial is opposed to the spirit of the age. Believers who want to please God *and* enjoy a good life are asking for trouble. Our total devotion must be to one or the other. In order to live a holy life that is pleasing to God, we must resist the spirit of the age and serve Jesus wholeheartedly. According to Jesus, the break must be so complete that we actually die to the world's system. Jesus calls for total and

radical commitment from those who would save their lives
from the spirit of the age.

"God Wants to Fill Your Life
with Good Things"

Were the 12 disciples attracted to Jesus because of the
"good things" He had to offer them? Luke records the
account of a man who said to Jesus, "I will follow you
wherever you go." Jesus answered him, "Foxes have holes,
and birds of the air have nests; but the Son of man has
nowhere to lay his head" (Luke 9:57,58). We don't hear
those verses preached very often because they don't support the doctrine that promises a life full of good things.

We believe that God is kind, loving, and generous, so
we feel constrained to find a way for God to bless us in
terms our materialistic world will understand. We skip
over Luke 9:57,58 and make John 10:10 our rallying cry: "I
came that they may have life, and have it abundantly."
Abundant life sounds a lot better than not having a place
to call home. Abundant life suggests to us that we can
follow Christ and fulfill our own desires for good things at
the same time.

And why shouldn't we seek both? Why indeed?
Because Jesus said, "No one can serve to masters.... You
cannot serve God and mammon [money, material things]"
(Matthew 6:24). Then He commanded, "Seek first his
[God's] kingdom and his righteousness, and all these
things shall be yours as well" (Matthew 6:33). If we ignore
the fact that on judgment day we will give an account of
how we have lived, we will set our hearts on filling our lives
with good things. But Paul warned against this kind of
thinking: "There is great gain in godliness with content-
ment; for we brought nothing into the world, and we
cannot take anything out of the world; but if we have food
and clothing, with these we shall be content. But those
who desire to be rich fall into temptation, into a snare, into

many senseless and hurtful desires that plunge men into ruin and destruction" (1 Timothy 6:6-9).

The difficulty at this point is being balanced between the good life and the God life. I could try to compensate for the overemphasis on prosperity in American Christianity by denying God's desire to bless His children spiritually, emotionally, and physically. But the truth is that God *does* prosper those who put Him first. The danger occurs when the *result* of God's goodness—physical and material prosperity—becomes the *object* of our desire.

American Christians also seek the rewards of the good-life gospel because we recognize that God has blessed America materially. The good life and God's blessing seem to fit together quite naturally. But God hasn't blessed us because we are more deserving than other nations. It is ironic that many believers who would never think of themselves as better than others on an individual level are deluded into thinking that our nation is better than all the others. They recognize the dangers of personal pride, but they are guilty of national pride.

America is not the best nation on the planet. Every nation is special to God in its own unique way, just as each one of our children is special in his or her own way. Different nations have fulfilled different roles in history, but no nation has a corner on the covenant of God's blessing. Each nation, including America, must give an account for its sins. God plays no favorites with individuals or nations.

I have struggled personally with finding the right balance on the question of prosperity. Several years ago my wife and I started talking together about our desire to have a home. We had lived in rented apartments and missionary housing for 23 years, and the desire to have a home of our own was strong. Though we live overseas, we talked about how wonderful it would be to have a house and a few acres in the mountains to call our own.

But the more we talked, the more I was overwhelmed with confusing thoughts: Have I compromised my life as a minister and a missionary? Am I getting entangled in worldly pursuits? Am I negotiating my call to preach the gospel?

One day, after weeks of struggling, it dawned on me that my desire to build a home for my family might be from the Lord. "Could this really be You, Lord?" I cried out. "If so, please send someone with a word from You. I desperately want to know if my desire is from You, Lord Jesus."

Two days later I spoke in a church in Lakewood, California. The pastor's wife approached Sally and me after the Sunday meeting. "I have been burdened for you all week," she said. "The strangest thought keeps going through my mind. I have prayed over and over that God would give you a home here in America, something that is yours personally, a retreat for your family. I believe God wants to give you a home you can come back to some day."

I couldn't believe my ears! The answer to my prayer came so quickly and was so specific.

In a matter of weeks we purchased a beautiful five-acre parcel of land in the mountains of Southern California. Two years later we obtained a bank loan and built a beautiful log home. It has a small apartment downstairs which we open up to friends as a retreat site. We're also able to make it available to my parents who recently retired after 45 years of pastoring.

Though we still live overseas on a full-time basis, we love our home in the mountains. It is God's gift—a material gift—and we are thankful. We didn't seek it, but as we served Him and sought Him, He provided the desire of our hearts.

We learned through this experience that it is not wrong to own nice things as long as they don't own us. And we learned not to consider our home as a sign that God loves us more than He loves our friends in Africa or Latin America.

I can't base my theology of God's love on material blessings. We don't deserve our home in the mountains any more than a poor pastor in Ethiopia deserves a home to live in. I just see it as a wonderful gift from God, and I am deeply thankful.

"God Wants to Bless Your Business"

Jesus saw Matthew sitting at the tax collector's table. He said to him, "Follow me." Immediately Matthew put down his accounting books, arose, and followed Jesus (Matthew 9:9). As Jesus was walking by the Sea of Galilee, He saw two brothers—Peter and Andrew—casting their nets into the sea. He called to them, "Follow me, and I will make you fishers of men." Immediately the two left their nets, their obvious livelihood, and followed Jesus (Matthew 4:19). Further on the three of them came upon James and John in a fishing boat. Jesus called to them also, and they rowed ashore, waved goodbye to their father, and followed Jesus as well (Matthew 4:21,22).

How would these five disciples have answered the question, "Did Jesus help your business prosper?" I can just imagine Peter saying, "Well, catching men is okay, but they don't fetch the same price at the market that my fish used to!" Or perhaps Matthew would have answered, "Yes, I'd have to say Jesus set me free from all my business worries—and my business as well!"

Those who think that a commitment to Christ automatically means He will make their businesses successful couldn't prove it by the experiences of the early disciples. Jesus does call some of us to remain in our businesses and causes those endeavors to flourish, but not because we deserve His blessing. He blesses us because He is merciful.

Many people in business have forsaken all and followed Jesus by serving Him in another land. That's their calling. For these people, their vocation is their mission field. They are "full time" for Jesus, and He blesses them.

Contrary to what the good-life gospel proclaims, Jesus' primary concern for us is not enhancing our business, improving our weaknesses, or helping us achieve the goals we have set for ourselves. His concern is that we make *Him* our primary concern. As Paul put it, "I press on toward the goal for the prize of the upward call of God in Christ Jesus" (Philippians 3:14). The real issue at stake is, should the Master bid, "Arise, come forth, and follow me," are we prepared to forsake our businesses and follow Him?

"It's Your Right to Be Blessed"

Something doesn't ring true about this statement. Doesn't the Bible say something about laying down our rights? According to Scripture, we're bondservants of Christ, and a bondservant in biblical days had no rights.

Paul exhorted, "Have this mind among yourselves, which you have in Christ Jesus, who, though he was in the form of God, did not count equality with God a thing to be grasped, but emptied himself, taking the form of a servant.... Therefore God has highly exalted him" (Philippians 2:5-9). Some believers want the exaltation without the humiliation, the blessing without the sacrifice, the resurrection power without the crucifixion agony. But as Christ's servants, we have no rights.

The doorway to God's blessing is holiness. Each blessing He gives is not necessarily a response to our faith, but an expression of His faithfulness. Every good gift we have received is undeserved. Paul told the Corinthian Christians, "What have you that you did not receive? If then you received it, why do you boast as if it were not a gift?" (1 Corinthians 4:7). In fact, it is dangerous to demand from God what we deserve. Don't demand it—you might get it!

At the heart of the good-life gospel is a demanding, self-seeking attitude promoted by the spirit of the age. It is a me-first philosophy that undermines godly living and sacrificial service. This me-first spirit is destroying our nation because it promotes selfishness. It will ultimately lead to God's judgment on our nation unless we recognize it for what it is and turn back to God.

Do you struggle to experience spiritual victory in your life? Perhaps you have been influenced by the spirit of the age more than you realize. I encourage you to offer your life and all you possess to Jesus *right now.* Pledge to obey him. Make yourself available for sacrificial service, anywhere, anytime, for any task. If you cannot do this freely, it is a sure sign that you are caught by the spirit of the good life and you need to break free. As you do so, you will be prepared to overcome another, and perhaps even more deceptive servant spirit of Satan: American individualism.

—8—
Alone in a Crowded World

There has always been a rugged and well-proven individualism at the heart of American society. Though a great strength when devoted to the glory of God, American individualism turns into a powerful force for evil when it is divorced from biblical Christianity. A nation hacked out of the wilderness by rugged individualists and rags-to-riches immigrants can turn into a nation of egotists if this pioneering energy is not devoted to the Lord Jesus.

Individualism is as American as hot dogs, baseball, apple pie, and motherhood. Indeed, Americans cherish as sacred their right to life, liberty, and especially the pursuit of happiness. For individualistic Americans, anything that stands between us and thinking for ourselves, working for ourselves, living for ourselves, judging for ourselves, and voting for ourselves is seen as sacrilegious, a violation of our most basic rights.

American individualism emerged more than 200 years ago from our struggle against aristocratic authority which imposed tea taxes and denied our basic rights to private ownership of property, individual representation, and religious freedom. Our is a hard-won individualism, and it is now nurtured and jealously guarded by the family, the community, the church, educational institutions, and government.

Self Above Society

But now we face a great dilemma in our nation. Modern individualism, which is divorced from the moral foundations of Christianity and surrounded by a hedonistic society, has produced a way of life that is neither beneficial to individuals nor productive to society at large. Individualism used to be expressed positively within the context of the family, the community, the church, and the government. Personal rights were subjected to the overall good of society. But individualism today no longer observes such boundaries. The cry is, "I want what I want when I want it!" Such selfish individualism weakens the very underpinnings of a nation built on strong moral foundations. In his book *Habits of the Heart*, Robert Bellah points out that individualism in which self has become the main focus cannot be sustained.

As a result of the rise of self-centered individualism in our nation, the social structures to which individuals held themselves accountable are now crumbling. For example, the traditional American family and its values are vanishing. Not only has selfish individualism created alienation between children and their parents, but also between adults and their parents. Adult children taking responsibility for their aged parents has been an accepted family obligation throughout history. But now many Americans scoot the elderly off into retirement centers and geriatric wards to await their impending doom. Not only is this an ignominious end for the elderly, but often their care is at the financial expense of the state. "Out of sight, out of mind" fairly well describes the attitude of many people toward parents who are an inconvenience to their children's fun-filled, self-centered lives.

Individualism is also disintegrating the community. "Alone in the crowd" aptly describes the effect of individualism in our cities and neighborhoods. Americans have lost the art of and the need for relating to others on anything but a cursory level. Instead of community interdependence, satiation of personal desire has become the paramount driving force in American life.

In the movie *Crocodile Dundee*, the title character, who has lived all his life in the Australian outback, makes a naive observation as he's driven through the streets of New York City for the first time: "Seven million people live here, aye? Must be a real friendly place then." Anyone who has been to New York knows differently! It's not the accumulation of people in a geographic area that makes it a friendly place, but the way those people produce deep and meaningful relationships.

Individualism is also affecting the time-honored institutions of our society. Government leaders, in their quest for power, have lost the respect of the people. Education is no longer regarded as the means for preparing for a life of meaningful service to society. Rather it is viewed as a springboard into the job market where one can grab a share of the nation's wealth.

Robert Bellah and his associates concluded that a vast number of Americans have lost their sense of community and social obligation. To most Americans the world is a fragmented place that presents them with a multitude of choices and offers little meaning or comfort. They believe they are basically alone and have to answer only to themselves. Thus they find it very difficult to commit themselves to others. Left without God, the individual's pursuit of happiness and security is the only source of meaning.

Individualism turned loose on America without the restraints of family, church, and neighborhood is destroying our nation. The bottom line of the Pro-Choice Movement is the freedom of a mother to take the life of her unborn child if pregnancy or parenting is "inconvenient" for her. When the individuals in this nation cherish the freedom to do what they want to do above the responsibility to do what they ought to do, America is doomed.

Getting Back to Our Roots

The roots of modern, anchorless individualism can be traced to Enlightenment philosophers who removed God from the center of the universe and replaced Him with man. The following quote summarizes the beliefs of "enlightened" man with regard to God and morality:

> If we go back to the beginning...we shall find that ignorance and fear created the gods; that weakness worships them; that credulity preserves them; and that custom respects and tyranny supports them in order to make the blindness of men serve its own interests. Belief in God...is bound up with submission to autocracy, the two rise and fall together; and "men will never be free till the last king is strangled with the entrails of the last priest." The earth will come into its own only when heaven is destroyed.[1]

With God pushed out of the center of life, the needs and desires of people became the paramount guiding principle of morality. British philosopher John Stuart Mill (1806-1873) wrote, "The only freedom which deserves the name is that of pursuing our own good in our own way."[2] With moral absolutes overturned, man entered a relativistic world where the only thing left to guide him was himself.

The 1960s was a watershed decade for individualism in American history. It was the decade in which America lost its innocence. The moral underpinnings had already been eroded, but there was a lingering innocence about American greatness. However, in those years, people moved quickly from questioning the ethics of American involvement in the Vietnam war to questioning ethics in general. Biblical ethics and morality were held up to public scorn while "Turn on, tune in, and drop out" and "If it feels good, do it" became the prevailing ethic for many American youth. Songs admonished, "If you're not with the one you love, love the one you're with." Any pretense that we were a Christian nation was lost in a haze of marijuana smoke and grinding rock music. People were free to pursue their own individual pleasures. All that mattered was personal happiness. The break of an entire generation from Christian morality became public and final.

The Goal of Individualism

The rise of selfish individualism in our nation has pushed hedonism to the center of American society. Hedonism is defined as the belief that personal pleasure should be the main aim of an individual's life. Since the popularization of Hugh Hefner's "playboy philosophy" in the '60s, we have tended to associate hedonism mainly with sex and licentiousness. But hedonism's attachment to American society is broader than the sexual dimension. The American dream is basically a hedonistic dream. The goal of the American dream is the accumulation of material wealth and the upward social mobility that wealth brings. The hidden assumption behind the American dream is that wealth and status are our rights and that they will bring personal happiness, pleasure, and recognition.

The American advertising industry bombards the average consumer with 1,500 commercial messages a day promising success. These messages appeal to our fear of failure and of being left out of the American dream. We know what we want in America—material success and emotional happiness—and we think we know how to get it.

Hedonism is expressed by any deliberate action taken to possess something for the sole purpose of personal pleasure and the satiation of desire. The thing to be possessed may be material—such as a boat, a sports car, or a home entertainment center, or it may be a person desired for the purpose of sexual gratification. Americans have never been busier fulfilling their hedonistic dreams than they are today. What we possess has become the standard by which we measure one another's value as individuals.

If the things we possess make a statement about the kind of individuals we are, it is not surprising that people in America are paying more and more exorbitant amounts of money to make that statement. Someone recently shelled out $12.1 million for an antique writing desk, and $4.6 million was tendered for an antique table. Ultimately, however, hedonism is not about the price we pay for the objects we desire. It's about the desire which focuses our energy on possessing those objects. Most of us have no great desire to possess a $53.9 million Van Gogh painting. But we do yearn for a nicer house, a flashier car, or the latest model big-screen television. We may not lust after an internationally famous movie star, but we may experience the same kind of desire for a neighbor's spouse or a coworker at the office.

When we finally possess the thing we desire, we tell ourselves, we shall experience pleasure and happiness at last. Unfortunately, this is not so. Chasing pleasure for pleasure's sake is like looking for the proverbial pot of gold at the end of the rainbow. The new "toy" may bring pleasure for a moment, a few days, a few weeks, or even a few months, but soon we tire of it. The new house isn't all it's cracked up to be. The new car isn't much more exciting to drive than the old one. The new romantic partner has character flaws just like the former partner. Hedonism perpetuates desires which are never really fulfilled, resulting in a frustrating, never-ending quest for happiness.

Living a Compartmentalized Life

Selfish individualism also leads to compartmentalization of life. A person has his job, his family, his church, his club, and his recreation. Selfish individualism produces a Jekyll-and-Hyde syndrome in which a person's ethics and behavior change as he moves from one compartment of life to another, based on what he wants out of each setting.

For example, when a businessman is at home with his family, security, love, and togetherness are the expedient values. He gets what he wants out of family life when he is a loving, protecting husband and father. But when he is at the office the next day, making a deal, turning a profit, and climbing the corporate ladder become the expedient values. Now the warm and loving family man is prepared to deceive, bully, harangue, or cajole his customers, or even sleep with a business associate, if it will help him get what he wants out of work. Caught in a compartmentalized, relativistic maze, he becomes a moral chameleon, changing to suit the expediencies of the particular compartment he is in.

The end result of this selfish individualism is frustration, alienation, and despair. People were not designed by God to live as moral chameleons. If they persist in doing so, they will take a psychological battering in the form of disgrace, hurt, broken relationships, and shattered lives. Unfortunately, such experiences have become the daily fare of contemporary American society.

"Privatizing" Our Faith

Christians also get caught up in the hustle-bustle spirit of selfish individualism. We get so busy making our mark on the world that we cut ourselves off from vital

Christian community and accountability. Jesus is Lord of our church life, but not Lord of all of life. We become part of the same get-ahead way of life that characterizes our neighbors and peers.

Selfish individualism has always been built on the claim that we have a right to our own lives and to see things from our point of view. The spirit of modern individualism has so infiltrated the thinking of American Christians that it has isolated believers in a kind of privatistic Christianity. Though it sounds quite pious and acceptable to say that religion is a "personal thing," it's not true. Individualism in the church is a dangerous illusion. Christians are to stand against the world, but never alone. *Together* we are to discern evil in the culture around us. We must work out our response to it through *corporate* Bible study, prayer, and discussion. The consequence of privatized faith is that our credibility and spiritual authority is thwarted in the public arena.

Yet we struggle to find the time and strength to fulfill our Christian responsibility of church attendance each week, much less the time for meaningful involvement in the lives of other believers. After a long day of fighting through hectic traffic jams, struggling to maintain a Christian witness in an antagonistic work environment, and shopping on the way home from work, the exhausted believer hardly feels like fellowshipping with other Christians. The pressures and structures of our modern society pull believers toward a private way of living.

Television supplements this new brand of Christian individualism by serving us spiritual nourishment and Christian entertainment at our convenience. Television reinforces our right to a private faith without the obligations that go with human relationships. When you are offended by the pastor or confused by a church split, the electronic church is there to minister to your need. It's all too easy to avoid the problems, conflicts, and responsibilities of church life by staying home and tuning in the TV evangelists and pastors. After all, if one of them offends you, you can pick up the remote control and "change churches" without even leaving your easy chair.

Back to the Cross

Individualism fragments and compartmentalizes our lives, limits our influence on the world around us, diminishes our desire to give our lives wholly to follow Christ, and contributes to a desire for anonymity. In contrast, Jesus beckons us to take up our cross and follow Him (Mark 8:34,35). This command confronts our self-seeking, pleasure-oriented American culture. Jesus tells us that unless we lose our life to Him and to others, we cannot find it.

To resist the pressure and power of the individualistic spirit of the age we must have a compelling reason to live the Jesus life. If we are to die to self and resist the tremendous pressure to let the world capture our time and energy and squeeze us into its mold, we desperately need to be close to Jesus and His people.

Holiness in an individualistic world means standing against the spirit of the age by refusing to privatize our lives. This is a difficult stand to take because American culture is such a rat race. The first step to being free is to recognize the spirit of selfish individualism for what it is and make a commitment to rise above it. Such a commitment is impossible without wholehearted devotion to Jesus and involvement with His church.

—9—
The Greed-Is-Good Syndrome

I n the 1988 hit movie *Wall Street*, the main character, a powerful financial tycoon named Gordon Gekko, personifies another servant spirit which has captured our nation and is negatively influencing Christ's church. At one point in the film, while trying to inspire his rapt underlings, Gekko says, "Greed is good. Greed is right. Greed clarifies, cuts through, and captures the essence of the evolutionary spirit. Greed—mark my words—will save the USA."

Greed hasn't saved the USA. Instead it has plunged her into billions of dollars of personal and corporate debt. In 1980 the United States was the world's largest creditor nation. Our country went into the red in 1985 and today is the world's largest debtor nation.

America has been swept away by the spirit of consumerism. In our devotion to the spirit of the age and our unbridled desire to have the best, the newest, the latest, the most advanced, the safest, and the most fashionable, our national motto has become "shop till you drop." One pundit described modern day consumers as those who buy things they don't need with money they don't have to keep up with people they don't like!

We joke about our rampant consumerism because we are embarrassed by our affluence. No doubt the extravagance of our wealth has made us not just a little self-conscious in a world of so much poverty.

I'm not saying that it is wrong to own property, purchase the goods and services we need, or succeed in private enterprise. I'm calling attention to an obsessive spirit in America: the drive to consume beyond the boundaries of need. I am warning against the greed-is-good mentality, a mentality which is pummeling America and the American church into spiritual softness.

A Change for the Worse

Around the turn of the century a fundamental cultural transformation occurred in the United States which gave rise to a spirit of rampant consumerism in our nation. National marketing experts actually identified and targeted for eradication such traditional values and institutions as the family, the Protestant work ethic, the savings mentality, and biblical morality. They knew that "to thrive and spread, a consumer culture required more than a national apparatus of marketing and distribution; it also needed a favorable moral climate."[1] Traditional American values were bulwarks against the tide of consumerism which had to be removed.

As a result of this transition, a crucial moral change occurred that facilitated the shift from a predominantly Christian influence to self-centeredness in our national culture. It was a shift from the Protestant morality of salvation through self-denial to "a therapeutic ethos stressing self-realization in this world."[2] A new distinguishing moral attitude began to emerge, one that massaged the ego and catered to the emotions of the individual. The character of America changed. People became preoccupied with preserving their own identity, health, and happiness. Once firmly entrenched, this new attitude provided fertile ground for the consumer society which today is in full bloom.

The experience of the Depression in the '30s added emotional energy to this process. Long work days, starvation wages, and overcrowded, pitiful work camps were common during that time. Our parents experienced the trauma of a decade of poverty which is incomprehensible to most of us born after World War II. Following the war the nation vowed never again to experience the horrors of poverty and war. As a result, many of us grew up with parents who worked hard so we would not suffer as they did. They determined that we should get a good education in order to get a good job and enjoy a good life.

The values of the baby-boomer generation have been shaped by these inherited reactions to the Depression. The consumer spirit was turned loose on America. Consumerism flourished in a nation that perceived itself to have inherited a divine destiny of prosperity.

The consequences of the consumer culture are tragic and many. The story of Barbara Hutton, the "poor little rich girl," illustrates what can happen to a love-starved individual in a consumption-mad society. Hutton became the heiress of the $50 million Woolworth fortune at age 12. But after seven marriages and a life of heartache, she died a lonely woman with only $3,000. She had everything the world considers important, yet she died lonely and frightened in a nation of lonely and frightened people. She discovered too late that the consumer culture can promise many things, but it can't deliver love. Loveless consumption is a mark of the spirit of the age.

The Mall Becomes a Sanctuary

The symbol of our culture's addiction to consumerism is the shopping mall. The mall has become a kind of secular cathedral, fulfilling a profound religious need in secular society for security, human contact, and closeness to the forces that shape our identity. It's not unusual to see people exercising in a mall, walking its perimeter under the protection of security guards. Nor is it unusual to find teenagers hanging out at the food courts and ice-skating rinks. The latest trend is to build amusement parks inside malls complete with water parks and roller coasters. The modern mall meets every need—or does it?

Architects like James Ross, who was the driving force behind Baltimore's Harbor Place, New York City's South Street Sea Port, Boston's Faneuil Hall, and more than 50 other malls and marketplaces, have consciously designed these centers with subtle religious themes. The presence of vegetation (symbolizing creation), fountains (symbolizing baptism), and light (symbolizing God) speak of man's basic spiritual nature. The mall in America is where we worship. But instead of worshiping God we give adoration to the latest fashions and countless other gods of materialism.

For James Ross, the mall is the democratic, unifying, universal gathering place which gives spirit and personality to the urban environment. The mall is where all people—rich and poor, old and young, black and white—come together, but not necessarily to buy. Surveys show that over 40 percent of those who come to shopping malls do not plan to buy anything (yet 90 percent of them *do* buy something). It is a community center of sorts that provides a focus for human contact. The mall has replaced the church as the social and spiritual center of America. Unlike most churches, however, the mall is open seven days a week, providing for some Americans the greatest sense of community they can experience.

Perhaps the mall experience does help people transcend many of the differences found in American culture. But does it really fill the emptiness of our time? People may shop till they drop, but they will still leave the shopping center ultimately unfulfilled because consumerism does not meet the real needs of the human heart.

A Consuming Search for Meaning

In his book *Following Christ in a Consumer Society*, John Kavanaugh states that consumption and marketing are "the ethical lenses through which we are conditioned to perceive our worth and importance."[3] Not only has the spirit of consumption profoundly affected our self-understanding, but also our behavior. Many Americans believe that the more possessions they acquire, the happier they will be. They wrongly assume that the person who produces more, owns more, or performs better is most important.

Kavanaugh tells about a young girl named Amy who committed suicide. Her farewell note contained these sad words: "If I fail in what I do, I fail in what I am." Tragically, the forces shaping our consumer culture leave many people feeling they have no uniqueness or value. To be acceptable, to be beautiful, and to be loved is equated with the products we purchase and the clothes we wear. The "haves" express airs ranging from subtle conceit to intense snobbery toward the "have nots" who don't wear the trendiest clothes or the latest designer watch, don't carry the "in" purse, or don't drive the best car. With life's meaning being dictated by these material values, individual purpose is essentially defined in relation to what we can buy, sell, or possess.

Many young, upwardly mobile Americans have a desperate need to achieve a sense of meaning in life through consumption. If they can buy what they want and take it home to enjoy and display to their peers, they somehow feel affirmed as persons of value. This need to consume comes partly from a dread of being left out, of not having a good time. Ours is such a touch, feel, own, consume society that we are conditioned to feel a vague sense of insecurity if we don't spend money. Have you ever felt tired or discouraged and had the desire to feel better by going shopping? I have, and I have experienced tremendous conflict because of it. There are times I have felt an irrational desire to go to the mall or go shopping as a way of dealing with a bad day. I am a child of my own culture, and I don't like it!

While such feelings are difficult to chart, they are nonetheless pervasive in our society. This pull to shop ourselves into a good feeling is the fallout of a consumer culture. Society has become increasingly impersonal, and this impersonalness has created a mass feeling of inner emptiness. Sadly, we deal with it by going to the mall even when we don't need anything or plan to buy anything.

A Church Consumed

A close look at the church in America reveals that Christians have been deeply influenced by the spirit of consumerism. The household of God has been turned into a warehouse for Christian loot. The Sunday morning gathering of believers is often more a fashion show than a time to meet the Lord. Instead of being at odds with mammon as we are taught by the Lord Jesus, we have welcomed the money changers back into God's house. We have created a sacramental materialism in the name of Christ. Church growth has become big business. The evangelical movement has become the evangelical market.

No one is as worldly as evangelicals when it comes to direct mail and the methods of Madison Avenue. A friend of mine who is the pastor of Christ Our Shepherd Church in Washington, D.C., recently received a computerized fund-raising letter from a Christian organization. The computer had mistakenly inserted the church's name where the pastor's should have been. Thus the letter began with "Dear Mr. Christ" and continued "Mr. Christ, we would appreciate your gift..." The irony of this case of mistaken identity lies in the fact that Jesus was being solicited in a "personalized" computer-generated letter to support what He has already purchased with His blood.

By assimilating the methods of the world, the church has opened its doors to the spirit of consumerism. As a result, many of us are becoming weary of junk mail advertising Christian book and record clubs, magazines, inspirational cruises, and seminars for every topic imaginable. We've grown cold to incessant appeals for money on Christian radio and television programs which face a new financial crisis every month. We've become disillusioned by the lavish waste of our sacrificially given, designated offerings which are lining the pockets of those who minister instead of touching those in need of ministry. We are inundated with what some call "holy hardware" or "Jesus junk," a seemingly endless stream of plaques, bumper stickers, T-shirts, jewelry, buttons, bookmarks, etc. The commercialization of Christianity signals that we—those of us who sell and those of us who buy—have been seduced by the spirit of the age.

We've not only succumbed to consumerism within the Christian subculture, but outside it as well. Most Christians are no different in their buying habits than anyone else in the world. Not only do we fill our homes with more books, tapes, and holy hardware than we need, we also part with our money for all the trappings of what the world identifies with the good life: VCRs, hot tubs, health club memberships, lavish wardrobes, etc. Buying and selling goods per se is not the problem. It's the consumer spirit behind it that should alarm us.

The Value of Holiness

When we American Christians return to holiness, our economic values will be affected. Subsequently, the church will feel the repercussion of millions of evangelicals repenting from the "shop till you drop" mentality. When evangelism and missions become our passions we will have plenty to do to fill the idle hours we now spend in malls and shopping centers. When we turn away from the spirit of consumerism, I wonder if we will not feel ashamed about the extravagant amounts we have spent on church complexes, pipe organs, lavish furnishings, and huge pastoral salaries. I'm convinced that much of the money tied up in the material trappings of the church could be better used to care for our nation's poor and homeless.

Families will also experience repercussions when the spirit of consumerism is broken. When need replaces greed as our standard of living, some parents will be able to quit their second jobs and spend more time with their children. When our focus is turned from the material to the eternal, some believers will begin to covet their neighbor's prayer life instead of his Mercedes. When a revival of holiness comes, desperate appeals for donations will peter out. Faith ministries will begin to operate on faith, and dead works will be exposed for what they are.

America desperately needs God, and the church needs Him even more. The spirit of consumerism gripping this nation can be broken, but it will not happen until judgment begins in the household of God.

— 10 —
Option Fatigue

Two Russian pastors recently visited the United States. One of them needed a toothbrush, so their host, a friend of mine, took them to a local supermarket. The two Russians were staggered by what they saw: aisle after aisle of shelves bulging with groceries. There wasn't just one shelf of cereal, but many shelves stocked with dozens of different brands of cereal. Not only were there enough apples in the bin to feed everybody in their Russian town, but there were oranges, bananas, grapes, and exotic fruits of all kinds.

When my friend took them to the toiletry section to buy the toothbrush, they found a special sale: "Buy one and get one free." The two pastors were accustomed to waiting in long lines during freezing weather just to buy bread and meat. They felt fortunate if the food supplies were not exhausted before their turn came to buy. But now they faced a rack bulging with more than 20 different brands and colors of toothbrushes. The poor pastors not only had to select one toothbrush from the confusing variety, they also had to select the free toothbrush as well! They were so overwhelmed with the variety and abundance before them, they found it difficult to make a selection.

Decisions, Decisions, Decisions

The experience of these two Russian pastors illustrates another dilemma which is characteristic of the spirit of the age. I call it option fatigue. Not only are we an affluent, consumption-driven culture, but because of it we must wade through an overwhelming multitude of choices every day at all levels of life. On election day you must choose between a number of candidates representing different political parties. When the gas tank is low, you must decide which oil company to patronize, regular or super, a fill-up or $5 worth. And on such a simple matter as buying an ice cream cone, you must choose from a tempting array of 31 flavors! Though in many ways such freedom is a blessing, option fatigue exacts a staggering toll on the American population.

I can remember coming home from a long day of work and saying to my wife, "Sally, I am so tired of making choices. Would you please choose where we will go out to eat tonight?" I couldn't stand to make one more choice.

The option fatigue we encounter in America reflects another servant spirit of the age: option excess. The most damaging area of life in which this spirit operates is the area of moral and spiritual values. Our forefathers established America as a land where the God of the Bible could be worshiped freely and openly. But the Christian value system upon which our nation was founded is no longer the primary moral force in our society. The influences of atheism and liberalism have undermined our national belief in God and the Bible. Moral and spiritual values are now seen as relative instead of absolute. People still believe in right and wrong, but only as they, not God, define it.

When the dynamics of moral relativism and option excess meet as they do in our culture, it's like striking a match in a room full of gas fumes. Why? These two spirits are explosive because people are free to make their own moral choices without the benefit of sound moral guidelines.

The abortion issue is a prime case in point. Before the acceleration of choices most women who became pregnant—whether the pregnancy was planned or not—carried their infants to term and gave birth. Abortion was murder; any woman choosing an abortion was looked upon as a murderer.

Today, however, moral relativism allows for a number of interpretations of the abortion issue: all abortions are murder, some abortions are murder, no abortions are murder, etc. And the spirit of option excess affirms every woman's "right" to decide the morality of taking the life of her unborn child. The social and legal upheaval our land is experiencing today over the abortion issue can be traced directly to our having too many options with no moral guidelines. The same explosive possibilities attend the intersection of moral relativism and pluralization in such issues as premarital and extramarital sex, homosexuality, euthanasia, and genetic engineering. The right to make choices regardless of how they affect others is not the kind of freedom the writers of the Constitution had in mind.

Choices in the Church

Obviously, having the opportunity to make choices is not in itself wrong. God created us with free will. Christianity is a religion of choices. Protestantism was born as a protest and, as Os Guinness states, "Thus the Christian gospel always insists on an alternative perspective, and as such is a generator of choices and dissent. This, as we have seen in the past, is the source of its socially disruptive power."[1] Christianity has created by its existence a basis of intellectual creativity and moral opportunity. It has contributed to the process by which the number of choices is ever increasing for individuals in our society.

However, the number of choices we must make daily, and the emotional and spiritual energy expended to make them, undermines our Christian faith in significant but often indiscernible ways. It takes an unbelievable amount of energy just to survive in America because we must deal daily with so many choices. Guinness continues:

> Life is now a smorgasbord with an endless array of options. Whether a hobby, vacation, lifestyle, worldview, or religion, there's something for everybody—and every taste, age, sex, class, and interest. The church of your choice? A liturgy to your liking?...The "Good Food Guide" has its counterpart in the "Good Church Guide." Pass down the line; take your pick; mix your own; do your thing.
>
> We have reached the stage in pluralization where choice is not just a state of affairs, it is a state of mind. Choice has become a value in itself, even a priority. To be modern is to be addicted to choice and change. Change becomes the very essence of life.[2]

The emphasis on free choice and easy change contributes to shallowness and hypocrisy in the church. Picking and choosing are the order of the day. Marilyn Monroe once said, "I just believe in everything—a little bit."[3] Her attitude is not too different from that of many church-hopping, conference-attending, television-watching Christians. Spirituality has become a smorgasbord affair for them. The transition from this brand of spirituality to a kind of morality-buffet approach to the important decisions of life is not a difficult one to make.

The Fallout of Too Many Choices

It is important to consider the consequences of the burgeoning array of options and choices in our culture. There may be others, but I have identified five.

1. An Increase in Choices Leads to a Decrease in Commitment

Christian commitment today is like Teflon: it doesn't seem to stick to anything. Believers change marriage partners and jobs for the flimsiest of reasons.

Christians also have problems with their commitment to other believers. If we don't like the preacher, the choir, or the youth program, we're tempted to bail out of the church rather than tough it out and pray it through. And the bigger the church, the easier it is for us to avoid commitment.

2. Option Abundance Leads to Boredom

Constant change leads to option addiction. Who hasn't been amazed by a teenager who complains of being bored after a family outing to Disney World or the zoo? Change becomes an end in itself for those too immature to realize their intellectual and creative poverty. This is the problem of an affluent society. While eastern European youth would be delighted and overwhelmed by a visit to one of our nation's smaller amusement parks, today's American kids are spoiled.

Christians in our culture are also spoiled. We are overwhelmed with an abundance of Christian teaching, churches, tapes, books, TV and radio ministries, retreats, counseling, and seminars. We have become spiritually obese by gorging ourselves on so much spiritual food. Boredom has set in for many Christians. The only way to cure this problem is to thrust ourselves into sacrificial service.

If we don't put what we know into action, we will turn to ever-increasing forms of entertainment to satisfy ourselves.

3. People Facing Too Many Choices Withdraw

People in America are so overwhelmed and fatigued from options that they withdraw in order to protect themselves. They turn inward instead of outward in order to survive. They long to escape the complexity of life. While some withdraw to "gated communities," others withdraw into alcohol and drug abuse.

4. Too Many Choices Result in a Throwaway Mentality

People have so many choices that they develop a kind of "disposable" attitude toward life. We enjoy so much abundance that we can throw away anything that we don't like, that's out of style, or that doesn't work right. Not only does this mentality lead to overspending, it also leads to superficiality in relationships. People tend to dispose of relationships in the same way they dispose of old clothes and used furniture.

Most non-Americans find this aspect of American culture repugnant. While we place exaggerated value on wealth and health, non-Westerners value family and friendship far more than prosperity. They take longer to build relationships, while we are quick to dispose of those we are "committed" to.

5. Too Many Choices Lead to a Desire for Anonymity

We long to get off mailing lists and away from telephone marketers. Americans want to escape the information bombardment that our computerized, technical world has created. We like the independence and anonymity that comes with attending big churches.

Choosing God's Way

How can we avoid the trap of overchoice and its devastating consequences? To do this is no simple matter. Christians must saturate themselves with God's Word. It is a lamp to our feet and a light to our path.

Many choices are forced upon us that we don't need to make. We don't need to order from the shopping channel or drop in at the mall three or four times a week. We can do with less variety in our menus. We don't need to have our hair done weekly. We don't need to subscribe to so many magazines. We can cancel the cable movie channel. As a result of many of these choices we will spend less money, requiring fewer working hours, allowing more time for life.

Another area in which we can simplify our choices concerns the church we attend. We can stop hopping from church to church, plug into one even though it isn't perfect, and be committed to the Christians we already know. This is what holiness means in a world ruled by a glittering array of choices. Believers must learn to make fewer choices and put more time and effort into the ones they do make.

Satan offered Jesus some wonderful options, but He refused to entertain the enemy's choices. He stayed with what His Father had given Him to do. He was single-minded. If we are to survive the option-filled world we live in, we must have the same determination. It is the only way to be holy in such a confusing world.

By fearing God, not people, and by knowing God's Word, we can resist the temptation to submit to the fads, fashions, and frills of modern life. Jesus is our rock. By walking in close relationship with Him we will easily see the superficiality of the vulgar, fashion-frenzied lifestyle prevalent in the church and the world.

Learning to hear God's voice and walk in His Spirit deepens our life and anchors us in the deep waters of spiritual growth. As a result we will become less active in worldly choices, but in the process we will become more like Jesus. There are choices that do not count in life, and these are the ones we want to avoid. Only one ultimate choice really counts, and that is who we trust to be our Lord. There are many idols, but only one Lord. There are many choices, but only one stands out above all the rest. When that choice is our priority and our spiritual sights are focused firmly on Jesus, we are ready to do battle against the spirit of the age.

— 11 —
The Great Cheerleader in the Sky

Years ago a person seeking to earn a private pilot's license had to pass a rather harrowing test of instrument flying. With the plane flying at about 10,000 feet, the instructor ordered the novice to pull back on the stick and point the nose straight up. This produced a stall, and the plane plummeted out of control in what is called a "graveyard spin." The only way for the student pilot to pull out of the spin was to fly by the instruments. In those days the novice even wore blinders to help him fight off the instinctive desire to look out the window in search of the elusive horizon.

Under the influence of the spirit of the age, our culture is like an airplane in a graveyard spin. We're out of control. The only way we are going to pull out of the dive is to get our eyes back on God. Sadly, the very instrument which God has ordained to redirect the nation's focus to God—His body, the church—is also in a spin. Jesus is no longer the center of the church's focus. We want His blessing but not at the price of giving up the worldly comforts we have come to prize so highly.

We have relegated the Lord Jesus to the role of cheer-leader. We want him on the sidelines cheering us on, but we don't want Him as the captain directing our lives. We want His encouragement, His guidance, and His help as long as He stays on the sidelines. We want His rousing cheers not His demanding discipline. We want the warm pat on the back and the affirming "well done," but we don't want Him to take absolute control of our lives. We believe in Jesus; we just don't want Him telling us how to live. The spirit of the age has pushed God to the margins of our busy lives.

A Nation Off Center

The greatest danger we face in America is not that people don't believe in God, but that they believe in God without allowing Him to rule their everyday affairs. Faith in God is up, but obedience to God is down. Polls reveal that almost 80 percent of the people in America believe in God, and that one out of every three Americans claims to be born again. Yet the impact of Christian faith on moral, social, and political life in America is diminishing. There is a great increase in crime, homosexuality, corruption, and substance abuse. Americans have never had so much religion and so little of God. We have more money to use, more technologies at our disposal, and less commitment to living out the gospel.

Through the process of industrialization and the influence of the Enlightenment philosophers, God has been gradually eased away from the center of society. Religion is symbolically important, but practically irrelevant. Modern society has become so diverse that the Christian religion has been reduced to being just one of many dimensions of our very busy and sometimes confusing lives. This compartmentalization of life has helped to displace God and religion from their rightful place at the very center of our society's existence. Os Guinness states that, starting from the center of life and moving outward, "successive sectors of society and culture have been freed from the decisive influence of religious ideas and institutions."[1]

Christianity has been essentially neutralized in America. We may still claim to be a Christian nation, but our historic Christianity no longer affects the way we live. The game of life goes on, but Jesus is not acknowledged the Lord of life. Most Americans are happy to have God somewhere on the sidelines, but they want to be the star players.

How have we crowded God out of the center? By replacing Him with ourselves. Human reason and intelligence make it increasingly easier for us to solve life's problems without God. We have manuals for reprogramming our personalities, making love, cooking, and winning souls. Life has been reduced to human know-how.

People still call out to God in times of tragedy, of course, from the foxhole in wartime to the stock market floor during a crash. But calling out to God when your family breaks up or when stock prices tumble or when the equity on your home is wiped out is not the same as allowing God to stand at the center of your life at all times and in every way.

A Neutralized Faith

As we have pushed God to the sidelines of life in our nation, Christianity as a force in society has been largely neutralized. The Christian faith is not denied; it is just not believed and lived. It is still important in terms of creating religious atmosphere, but its influence in the areas that are essential to integrity and character is far less effective. For example, most Americans don't mind that we have a chaplain in the senate or that a prayer is offered during the president's inauguration. But they don't want their leaders to get too serious about putting God in their politics. Christian influence in determining public policy has been removed, while Christianity as an organized religion remains fervent. God has been reduced to the level of the servant of society rather than the Lord of life.

The state of Christianity in the twentieth century compared with other centuries explains this phenomenon. Whereas in times past the number of Christians have been fewer, their impact has been greater because they insisted on obedience to their faith. Christians have historically applied the lordship of Christ to all of life. But stringent Christian obedience is largely a thing of the past. Christian religion is accepted as long as Christians don't moralize or get too pushy about obeying the Bible. But as Christians cease to obey the Bible, Christianity ceases to be a force in society.

Secularization and the Saints

Once Christ is removed from the center of our lives, becoming merely a consultant we turn to when we have problems, Christianity has been secularized. If Jesus is nothing more than a business partner for the businessman, a counselor for the married couple in trouble, and a good friend for the high school student, the door is open to secularization. Once Christianity is reduced to being a helpful but noncentral dimension of how we live, we are free to play on Sundays, divorce when we feel like it, and do anything we please as long as we give a token offering at church and support an orphan or two. Somehow, professing Christians have not made the connection that being a Christian should actually make a difference in how they live.

The spirit of secularization successfully invades the Christian life when religion is something we do on Sundays and when meaningful accountability to other believers is crowded out of our week by other "priorities." When lifestyle becomes more important than family life and work schedules push daily devotions into the twilight zone in our agenda, the spirit of the age has ensnared us.

If God truly stands center stage in our lives, every decision will be made in the light of eternity. The priorities of family life and God's call on our lives will dictate job choices and the pace at which we live. If Christ is Lord of all of life, we will gladly make lifestyle sacrifices to put God first. Our passions will be God's Word, prayer, fellowship, Christian service, learning to hear God's voice, growing in the faith, hungering for righteousness, and a childlike longing to know God and make Him known.

Holiness in a secularized world is not easy. Social religion is fashionable, but wholehearted obedience to God in every dimension of life is not. Such devotion smacks of fundamentalism, which can never be tolerated by those ensnared by the spirit of the age.

But we *are* to be a holy people. We *are* to live holy, humble lives, seeking God's divine wisdom and direction for every decision in life. Jesus is the Lord of all of life, the captain of the team. Every decision in life matters to God. There is no distinction between the sacred and the secular. Whether we eat pizza, play tennis, attend a Bible study, start a new business, or share Christ with a neighbor, everything we do is to be done for His glory.

PART 3

OVERCOMING THE SPIRIT OF THE AGE

— 12 —
Being Wholly Holy

How can we become the victors over the spirit of the age instead of its victims? I believe we will be victorious when we go on the offensive. There are two elements to every sport: defense and offense. You can keep from losing a game by playing defensively, but you will never win unless you go on the offensive. In order to conquer the spirit of the age in our hearts, our churches, and our nation, we must aggressively resist it by pursuing a life of holiness. That's what this part of this book is about.

It is not an easy task to find our way through the maze of secularization, individualism, consumerism, option excess, and the good life in our culture. While many practical and helpful ideas are presented in this section to help you live victoriously in this age, I must warn you that no list of ideas and no carefully devised plan of action can supplant knowing God in Jesus Christ. Jesus is "the author and finisher of our faith" (Hebrews 12:2, NKJV). Jesus is the One who will keep us from falling, and who will present us spotless before the presence of our Father (Jude 24). Holiness is first of all a relationship with Jesus Christ.

I urge you to read these chapters prayerfully, asking God to illumine the areas of your life which need to be regenerated or dealt with. We Christians are the building blocks of our society. As we overcome the spirit of this age through Christ and learn to walk in holiness, we will see people around us challenged, our churches renewed, and our political and educational institutions impacted. Jesus prayed concerning His disciples, "They are not of the world, even as I am not of the world" (John 17:16). May He also be able to say that of us.

How Not to Be Holy

There are many ideas about how to be holy and many of them are false. To some people the very word holiness brings images of long skirts, rule books, and clothes that are 20 years behind the time. To still others the idea of holiness is associated with "holier than thou" attitudes. Our cultural concepts of holiness are often a great hindrance to being holy.

I grew up in a denomination that handed people a 130-page rule book when they joined the church. The challenge for most of us as teenagers was not how to obey God, but how to obey that book. This put us off from godly holiness. We thought God was some kind of ogre sitting in heaven with a big stick, looking over the balconies of heaven, searching for those who enjoyed life. I had the idea that when He found me having fun or even daring to smile on a Sunday, He would reach over the balustrade of the heavenly balcony, beat me on the head with a stick, and yell, "Cut it out!"

For this reason many believers seem content to live a life of semiholiness. We know we aren't perfect, so some of us tolerate imperfection and failure. But the Bible was written so that we would be holy. God gave His law so that we would live without sin. If we are content to be "mostly holy" and sin "only a little bit," we have been seduced by the spirit of the age. Because God is holy, every sin is "an affront to God's authority, a disregard for his law, a spurning of his love."[1]

Some Christians find holiness unreachable, so they don't even try. They view themselves as "covered in the blood of Jesus," so they tolerate all sorts of compromise and disobedience. They use Jesus' death and the scriptural promise that we are covered by His blood to justify flagrant disregard of His grace. They mock God's mercy and presume upon His goodness and kindness.

For still others holiness is equated with the kinds of clothes they wear or things they do—or more accurately the kinds of clothes they *don't* wear and things they *don't* do. Still others equate holiness with ever-increasing levels of spiritual performance. Like the Pharisees they have endless lists of trivial do's and don'ts. In their view, each chapter in their book of regulations brings them a little closer to the bull's-eye of Christlike holiness.

But instead of making them more Christlike, the target concept of holiness produces self-righteousness. These Christians judge spirituality on the basis of outward performance. The person who attains a score of 300 on the performance scale is obviously more spiritual and more holy than the person who only reaches the level of 100. For these folk the ground around the cross is not level. There are tiers of attainment, and those reaching the higher tiers are obviously closer to God.

These concepts of holiness are repugnant to God because they are based on our good ideas of what we will and will not do for God. Holiness does not begin with man, but with God. It is not what we do for Him that makes it possible to be holy, it is what He has done for us. It is not how close we can get to Him that is the beginning point of holiness, but how close He has come to us. Holiness means to be separated from the world, set apart for God. We are able to be holy because He has promised to make us holy.

Our inability to obey the laws of God reveals to us our finiteness, our fallenness, indeed, our selfishness and rebellion against God. In the final analysis our greatest problem with holiness is not that our concepts of holiness are feeble, but that our hearts are rebellious. We are selfish; that's our problem. And the fact that we often won't admit our selfishness shows how deep the pride goes.

While God's law reveals our inability to live a blameless and holy life, God's grace makes it possible for us to do that which we fail to do in ourselves. We have no one to blame for our sin. Each one of us has ratified the rebellion of Adam against God's authority. We have each chosen to go our own way. Even the "nice people" in life are selfish. In my book, *The Father Heart of God* (Harvest House), I tell about a man I once met in India who said he had never sinned. Because of our mutual interest in religion, our casual conversation quickly turned to serious matters. When I shared that I believed God forgave those who acknowledged their sin, he asserted that he had never done anything wrong.

"You've never lied?" I asked him.

"No, never," came the answer.

"You mean you've never stolen something or hated someone?"

"No, not even once."

"Have you committed adultery?"

"No."

"Disobeyed your parents?"

"No."

"Did you ever cheat on an exam in school?"

"No, not that either."

I was baffled. Then I thought of another question. "Are you proud of the fact that you have never sinned?" I asked mischievously.

"Oh yes," he replied. "Very proud, very proud!"

"There you are," I said, "your first sin. You are a proud man!" He then laughed loudly and congratulated me that I had caught him in his only sin!

Though we are not all as proud as this man, we have all followed in Adam's original sin. Adam denied God's right to rule over his life, and he chose to go his own way. We have all made the same decision. It is hard for us to admit that we too have rebelled against God and denied His right to be Lord of our lives.

How to Be Holy

The first step to holiness which is acceptable to God is to be obedient to God's Word. The Bible not only commands us to be holy, but promises us God's enabling to obey Him and live in a manner acceptable to Him. The Bible contrasts holiness with idolatry and impurity (Romans 13:12-14) and evil desires (1 Peter 1:14-16). The Bible explains what it means to be holy. In 1 Samuel 12:20 we find the words, "Do not turn aside from following the Lord, but serve the Lord with all your heart." In Micah 6:8 the prophet says, "He has shown you, O man, what is good; and what does the Lord require of you but to do justice, and to love kindness, and to walk humbly with your God?" Everything we need to know about holiness acceptable to God is in His Word.

I believe we actually must go out of our way as believers not to be holy. Certainly the spirit of the age surrounds us, but if we seek God daily, read His Word, worship Him, and live a transparent life before our Christian brothers and sisters, sin becomes difficult! God so longs for us to be holy that He does all He can do short of robbing us of our free will to keep us close to Himself.

God expects from us an inward attitude of wholeheartedness that results in obedience. His first concern is the motivation of our heart. Is our heart set on pleasing Him? The requirements of the law are fulfilled in one word: love. We are to love God with all our heart. When our heart is fully intent on loving God, He sees our heart and accepts our longing to please Him.

We're talking here about wholehearted, loving obedience, not perfection. When I asked my son Matthew—a four-year-old at the time—to bring me a glass of water, he was a little clumsy, and he even stuck his fingers inside the glass! But he did succeed in doing what I asked. He wasn't perfect, but he was obedient. And the look of delight on his face, the knowledge that he wanted so much to please me, brought great joy to me as a father.

So it is with our Father in heaven. He does not accept disobedience or any form of impurity, but He rejoices in us when we want to please Him from the heart, even if our efforts are less than perfect.

Holiness that is acceptable to God is based on the heart. Man looks on the outward appearance, but God sees the heart (1 Samuel 16:7). Some teachings on holiness say we can never please God, that even our best efforts are defiled in the sight of God. But this is not the plain teaching of Scripture. We please the Lord when we sincerely do what He has asked of us.

The fact that we can please God does not imply we have achieved a state of sinless perfection. It does not mean that we can save ourselves by our good works. It just means God takes great delight in us as His children! Numbers 14:24 says of Caleb, "But my servant Caleb, because he has a different spirit and has followed me fully, I will bring into the land." Caleb pleased God because he followed God wholeheartedly. The psalmist David professed, "With my whole heart I seek thee" (Psalm 119:10). Because David followed God wholeheartedly, God called him a man after His own heart (Acts 13:22).

God never commands us to do something He will not enable us to do. We do not serve an unrighteous judge; God is fair. What He asks of us He makes possible. He does not command us to obey and then send us to hell for breaking the very laws which are impossible to keep in the first place. No one could respect a God like that. Our problem is not God's law. It's our refusal to obey God's law. But even in our selfishness God enables us to obey His Word if we are completely dependent on Him.

We become holy not because we can be perfect, but because God has all power. Even the most godly Christians have times of failure in the pursuit of holiness. The promise of Scripture is that moment by moment and day by day we can live a life that is pleasing to God. Nothing is too hard for God, including us! He is the One who enables us by His grace and power to obey Him. He has conquered sin on the cross, and He can conquer it in our lives as well.

Wholly Dependent on God

We can live a holy life if we acknowledge our total dependence upon God. If holiness means to be without sin, and God calls us to live in holiness, then as we live in dependence on God's grace hour by hour, he enables us to be free from sin. The key is to be dependent upon the Lord and accept His atoning sacrifice for us on the cross.

When we first came to Christ and accepted Him as our Lord and Savior, we were forgiven by God. He remembers our sins no more. We were made righteous in the sight of God because Jesus, through His death on the cross, took the punishment we deserve. Romans 5:1,2 tells us, "Therefore, since we are justified by faith, we have peace with God through our Lord Jesus Christ. Through him we have obtained access to this grace in which we stand, and we rejoice in our hope of sharing the glory of God."

Holiness is both a gift God imparts to us because of Christ's death on the cross and a process of daily sanctification made possible by the Spirit's work in our hearts. We are utterly dependent on God for both. We are justified, redeemed, and regenerated because Jesus took our sins and died in our place. When we trust in His atoning death for us, we are saved from our sins.

We must depend on God for daily holiness just as we depend on Him for salvation. Though we are made holy by the washing of His blood, we are still finite, fallen people who continue to grow in grace. This growth process is called sanctification. Though we will never be totally and infinitely holy as God is holy, we can be holy on the finite level by both accepting His work for us on the cross and by depending on the Holy Spirit to cleanse our hearts continually as He reveals those things in us that displease Him.

This is why the daily walk with God is so important. Relationship with our Lord Jesus is the heart of holiness. Knowing God as Father and growing in intimacy with Him is central to living a holy life. Holiness is not static; it's a dynamic relationship with the living God, our Father in heaven.

Making Holiness Your Goal

We Christians can be holy if we pursue God. If we want to know God more than anything else, God will see our hearts and will meet our desire. If we cultivate the passions of the Spirit by hungering for righteousness, God's Word, God's presence, and God's Spirit, the passions of the flesh will die. They will not rule over us. We're not talking about pursuing holiness for selfish gain but for the joy of knowing God. We're talking about surrendering our hearts totally to the Lord so that we can please Him by choosing to live for His glory.

Pursuing holiness requires an exercise of our will. There is a difference between our mind, our emotions, and our will. The Holy Spirit illumines our mind to understand truth, but it is with our will that we choose, by God's grace, to obey the truth. The mind contemplates, the will chooses, and the emotions follow.

Unfortunately for many people in our culture, the process works in the opposite order. People live by their feelings. Life is measured by how much self-gratification it brings the individual. But that's not the way to live a holy life. To be holy as He is holy we must set our mind on the truth and choose to obey the truth no matter how we feel. Our emotions can deceive us. The basis of righteousness and holiness is not our emotions, it is God's gift of salvation through the Lord Jesus. We choose holiness, not by doing what we feel but by doing the truth.

I can't overemphasize this truth. We live in a "feel-good" world. Ernest Hemingway said, "Good is what I feel good after, and bad is what I feel bad after." But if we live by our feelings we are giving in to the spirit of the age—the spirit of selfishness and self-gratification. Sadly, this spirit has invaded the church. Much of what passes for "having a good time" in worship experiences or conference settings is nothing more than the church conforming to the spirit of the age.

I believe in the joy of the Lord. It's a fruit of the Spirit. Those who live victorious Christian lives will experience great joy. But there is a difference between the godly joy which is the result of holy living and the selfish pursuit of good-time Christianity.

When this feel-good philosophy is carried directly from the world into the church, bypassing the cross and death to self, Christians cannot live holy lives. They are not willing to struggle against sin because such a struggle doesn't feel good! In fact, many young Christians are confused when, as new believers, their lifestyle of self-gratification suddenly comes into conflict with the Holy Spirit. It doesn't feel good! The habits of self-gratification are exposed, and a painful process of repentance and self-denial is begun. But if a godly Christian is not present to explain why this period of denial to self and to habits of self-gratification must be dealt with, the new believer may fall away. What is worse, carnal pseudo-Christians may come along and offer their brand of feel-good Christianity which is nothing more than a non-Christian lifestyle dressed up in Christian clothes. Nothing inside changes, and the confused young Christian continues to live by his feelings.

Holiness always confronts self-gratification. God calls us to turn away from living by our feelings and to live by the truth. Eventually we will receive emotional encouragement as a reward for obeying the truth. God created us with the capacity to feel. He intended our emotions to encourage righteous living. But he did not intend our emotions to be the basis of our choices. We pursue holiness by turning away from all forms of sin. As we turn away from the sins of the flesh, from lust, from covetousness, and from greed, God's Spirit conforms us to the image of Christ (Colossians 3:5-10).

The reward for denying self is the discovery of Jesus. We not only find Him to be our closest friend, but we become like Him. He lives within us. The more we seek Him, the more our hearts are consumed with a desire to know Him and be like Him. Jesus beckons us to flee the spirit of the age and run to Him. The complexity of life makes the alternative of pure and simple devotion to Jesus all the more appealing.

— 13 —
Pure and Simple Devotion to Jesus

here are times when the schedule of my life seems out of control. I tend to run from meeting to meeting, squeezing time with my family and friends in between them. My busyness all seems very logical and important: meeting with the kids' teachers at school, shopping, entertaining guests, leading a Bible study group, attending Sunday services, keeping up with business appointments, and the list goes on. I travel a lot, and that often complicates matters. Though I carefully plan my itinerary when I'm on the road, the unexpected almost always throws me a curve.

Then there is the telephone—or should I say telephones. Our two teenaged children each have their own friends who call at all hours of the day and night. And Sally and I need to keep in touch with our friends, so the phones in our home seem to ring incessantly.

I don't like living at such a frantic pace because the main priorities in my life—my walk with God and time with my family—often get squeezed out by lesser priorities.

A hectic lifestyle, full of pressure and busyness, undermines pure and simple devotion to Jesus. If we don't control our lives and our schedules we become puppets of the spirit of the age, yanked from one "important" event to another, constantly under pressure.

Several years ago things got so bad that Sally and I decided we needed to do something to regain control of our lives. During a family vacation we evaluated how busy we were and the consequences of our pace of life on our relationship with the Lord and each other. And we made changes—some simple, some drastic—with the express purpose of reserving time for the Lord and for each other. The process was so successful that we still evaluate our lives regularly to make sure our priorities are being met. It's a process I recommend to every family.

The first change involved the telephone. We bought an answering machine and added a second phone line. We keep the second line strictly for relatives and close associates. This allows us to turn off the main phone and still keep in touch with our family and be accessible in emergencies. This step required a lot of discussion with our teenagers. But they have come to appreciate our conviction that none of us can cultivate a holy life in a frantic household with constant interruptions.

The second step we took was to bring the television and the stereo, which ruled our home at one time, under the lordship of Christ. We had a couple of stormy sessions explaining concerns to Misha and Matthew. But when we asked them to pray about the influence of the TV and stereo on their lives, they finally agreed. We limited TV viewing to weekends, and only to programs Sally and I approved. We also decided that only Christian music would be played on the stereo.

The change that took place in our home was incredible. Our children both commented months later that establishing Christ's authority over the TV and stereo was a turning point in their walks with the Lord. And Sally and I were freed from an unhealthy dependence on the TV as a way to relax and unwind. We had more time for each other and for the Lord.

The third change we made concerned our schedule as a family, particularly my part of the schedule. We decided to plan our family calendar on a quarterly basis, setting aside certain weeknights at home together, days off, and other important events. We found that when we controlled our schedule, it couldn't control us. Best of all, we carved time into our lives for our pursuit of a simple devotion to Jesus.

Distracted from Devotion

In the New Testament account of Jesus' visit to the home of Lazarus, Mary and Martha were His hostesses for the day. Mary desperately wanted to be with Jesus, so she "sat at the Lord's feet and listened to his teaching" (Luke 10:39). But Martha was "distracted with much serving" (v. 40) and stayed busy making sure everything was proper. Jesus responded positively to Mary's longing to be with her Master by encouraging her devotion. And even though Martha did well, Jesus gently chided her, "Martha, Martha, you are anxious and troubled about many things. . . . Mary has chosen the good portion" (vv. 41,42).

We busy American Christians are like Martha. We are concerned about so many important things. What Martha was doing was important. After all, having Jesus in her home was not an everyday occurrence. We also are busy with much serving, and most of it is important: singing in the choir, PTA meetings, business dinners and appointments, and the list goes on and on. But Jesus also longs for us to choose the "good portion."

What is the good portion? Time with Jesus. It is so simple. The world is complex, but loving Jesus is not. He wants undefiled hearts attentive to Him, uncluttered minds waiting in His presence. He encourages us to spend unhurried moments in His Word, on our knees, and walking alone communing with Him.

No appointment, no business activity, and no church program is more important than time spent in the presence of the Creator of the universe. No dignitary or emissary is more important than Jesus.

It all comes down to what we esteem most important in life. How we spend our time is a reflection of what is most important to us. If Jesus is supreme to us, we will spend time with Him. Our values, ambitions, dreams, and aspirations will be centered on knowing and pleasing Him. If Jesus is our all-consuming passion, job security and achievement will come second.

How about it: Is He absolutely first in your life? Are you at peace in the knowledge that nothing or no one is more important to you than Jesus? Does your schedule reflect your love for Him? Or have other cares crowded Him to the margins of your life? Have you, like Martha, become anxious about many things? Or have you chosen the good portion as Mary did?

The greatest enemy of our devotion to the Lord Jesus is often religion itself. We can become so busy serving God that we have no time for the One we serve. The great Scottish revivalist Duncan Campbell once said, "Marching in God's army never makes up for time spent in God's presence." God created us for relationship. He did not create us to do things *for* Him, but to have relationship *with* Him. We are more important to the Lord Jesus than what we do for Him.

We are pulled away from devotion to Jesus by many pressures in our performance-oriented, action-packed world. Life is filled with pressures: work, school, kids, shopping, church, clubs, outings. When the day comes to an end and we feel spiritually empty, we know that our priorities are out of alignment.

I have suggested three steps to help you break out of this hectic, never-ending cycle of going and doing to make devotion to Jesus a priority. Are you willing to do anything necessary to regain control of your life and have the time and space you want and need to be devoted to the Lord Jesus? Are you willing to give up your house or your job if they stand in the way of undefiled devotion? Is there anything you are not willing to give up for Him?

If you are prepared to do anything to put your life in order and put Jesus first, then you can get serious with the Lord. Often the greatest barrier to undefiled devotion to Jesus is within us. It is the state of our hearts. We have become friends with the world (James 4:4). When being accepted by others and having a good job, a beautiful home, and nice clothes for the kids are more important than friendship with Jesus, we have allowed the spirit of the age to take root in our hearts.

Put Jesus First

The primary issue of devotion is lordship: Who rules your life? If Jesus is to be supreme, everything else must be second, including the nice, seemingly inoffensive things of the everyday world. There is nothing wrong with nice clothes for the kids, owning a car and a house, and having a good job. But when we get caught up in the spirit of the age and allow these things to capture us, they win our devotion. They creep slowly into a place of dominance in our lives. We soon find ourselves being controlled by these mundane, ordinary, nice things.

It sometimes takes a radical step to get our lives back under the lordship of Christ. It is important and necessary that you do whatever you must do to put Him first. I suggest that you start with a time of prayerful reflection over your values and ambitions. Set aside time to fast and pray. Ask God to forgive you for being caught up in the worldly spirit of running, buying, owning, and keeping up. Pledge your allegiance to His unqualified lordship.

Make whatever adjustments you need to make to put Him first. If it means cutting back on your work hours, do it. If it means selling your home and consciously choosing a simpler lifestyle so you will have the time you need to put God first, then act accordingly.

These kinds of decisions are acts of spiritual warfare, and they will be contested on all sides. Family and friends may think you're crazy. Your actions may be a threat to others around you. Don't try to justify your actions or condemn the lifestyles of others. Just obey God.

Putting God first is not a onetime event. It is a way of life, a process of growth and discovery. You will need to continually seek the Lord and lean on Him for His help and wisdom.

Seek Support

As you step out to establish a life of undefiled devotion to Jesus, it is essential that you find a group of friends in your church who are willing to support you in your new commitment. Pray with them regularly. Open up your life to them. Share with them your secrets, your fears, and your dreams. Be accountable. The very act of opening your life to others creates spiritual protection.

Furthermore, seek out a mature godly person, preferably a pastor or elder in your local church, and ask him or her to be your spiritual mentor. Ask this person to recommend books and tapes which will direct you in your spiritual growth. We all need a spiritual mother or a father in the Lord to help us along the way, as exemplified by Timothy's relationship with Paul (1 Corinthians 4:17).

Fear the Lord

In his book *The Practice of Godliness*, Jerry Bridges states that devotion to God consists of three elements: the fear of the Lord, the love of God, and the desire for God. Bridges writes, "The fear of God and the love of God form the foundation of true devotion to God, while the desire for God is the highest expression of that devotion."[1]

We don't hear much about the fear of God these days. It's a concept that seems somewhat old-fashioned and a bit harsh to most modern-day Christians. Yet it is a biblical concept, and it was not too long ago that we spoke commonly about "God-fearing people." Those who want to live in undefiled devotion to Jesus soon discover that one of the greatest hindrances to it is the fear of people. God's solution for this sin is that we put His fear in our hearts.

Some think that the fear of God is only an Old Testament concept, but that is not so. Although the concept is treated in greater depth in the Old Testament, references about the fear of the Lord are sprinkled throughout the Scriptures. Acts 9:31 reads, "So the church throughout all Judea and Galilee and Samaria had peace and was built up; and walking in the fear of the Lord and in the comfort of the Holy Spirit it was multiplied." Paul says the reason people rebel against the Lord is because "there is no fear of God before their eyes" (Romans 3:18).

What does it mean to fear the Lord? It does not mean trembling before Him in fright and dread. Rather, fearing God means that we hold God in such reverence that we hate what He hates. Proverbs 8:13 states, "The fear of the Lord is hatred of evil. Pride and arrogance and the way of evil and perverted speech I hate." Our hearts should be so in tune with Him and we should be so acquainted with His character that we loathe the shameful and evil things of this world.

Imagine that you arrived at church one Sunday morning to find that the sanctuary had been vandalized. Someone had piled manure and foul-smelling garbage on the communion table and the pulpit. Wouldn't you would feel angry, shocked, and repulsed by such a desecration of your place of worship?

That's how God wants you to feel about the sin in your heart. That's the attitude toward sin which the fear of the Lord will instill within you. You say you want your heart to be devoted to the Lord, pure and spotless. But when you allow bitterness, impure thoughts, lust, and greed to exist in your innermost being, you are allowing the manure and garbage of the world to defile the sanctuary of your heart. When you cultivate the fear of the Lord in your heart, you will begin to feel angry, shocked, and repulsed about your sin, and you will take steps to rid yourself of it.

Stand in Awe

The fear of the Lord is also defined in the Bible as reverence and awe of God. Psalm 96:3-6 reads, "Declare his glory among the nations, his marvelous works among all the peoples! For great is the Lord, and greatly to be praised; he is to be feared above all gods. For all the gods of the peoples are idols; but the Lord made the heavens. Honor and majesty are before him; strength and beauty are in his sanctuary."

It is impossible to be sincerely devoted to the Lord Jesus and not be filled with awe at His greatness and goodness. I sometimes read through the Psalms and underline verses which describe God's majesty and character. I then pray the verses back to the Lord, using them as a basis of worship and adoration. This process helps me focus on the Lord's greatness. Confessing aloud aspects of God's nature and character helps me reverence the Lord. It helps quiet my heart when I am surrounded by people and pressure.

Reverence for God means that He becomes more important to us than anything we might want to accomplish. God is looking for men and women who do not covet fame or fortune. Those who fear the Lord will not build themselves up. They will exalt the Lord Jesus. Paul wrote,

"He died for all, that those who live might live no longer for themselves but for him" (2 Corinthians 5:15).

God is searching for those in the body of Christ who aren't addicted to their own accomplishments. Many Christians are consumed with a competitive spirit, constantly seeking to outdo others in the church. Many pastors and evangelists worry that they will lose the support of the church if they do not produce a miracle a week. Only eternity will reveal how much the focus on human works has cost the church in true effectiveness.

To fear the Lord is to worship Him in our hearts for the majestic and awesome God He is. It is to acknowledge His holiness, power, wisdom, mercy, and splendor. It is finite man acknowledging the infinite God in all His goodness and greatness.

Focus on God's Love

In order to experience undefiled devotion to Jesus we must first understand that we are unworthy to receive God's love. We deserve to be punished for our sins. God is holy and we are sinful and deserve God's wrath. Furthermore, we must understand from our heart that even though we deserve hell, God loves us with everlasting love. We see His love when we look at the cross and see Jesus dying for our sins and offering us His righteousness (2 Corinthians 5:21).

A true picture of God's love captures our rebellious hearts and stirs us to undefiled devotion to Christ as nothing else can. The familiar painting of a meek and mild Jesus standing at the door of someone's heart and pleading to come in does not convey the staggering greatness of the love which motivated His death on the cross. He carried the sins of the whole world. He took the punishment we deserve and offers in its place forgiveness and new life. Nothing can subdue the heart of selfish men and women except the love of Jesus. He alone is without blemish, the spotless lamb of God taking the curse of sinful humanity on Himself.

The depth of our comprehension and appreciation for the love of God is conditional on how much we fear Him. We can't really love Him until we have a revelation of our own sinfulness and of what our sins have done to grieve the heart of God. Sin brings great sorrow to the Lord. Genesis 6:5,6 reads, "The Lord saw that the wickedness of man was great in the earth, and that every imagination of the thoughts of his heart was only evil continually. And the Lord was sorry that he had made man on the earth, and it grieved him to his heart."

It is difficult for us to understand the breadth of God's love for us. God's love never changes. It is not conditional on what we do or say. His love flows from His great heart of tenderness and mercy. His grace knows no boundaries. It is as great as the universe—and greater still! We are afraid that He cannot or will not forgive us when we consciously rebel against Him or do the terrible things we do which hurt Him and others. Yet God's love is so profound that Jesus died for our sins before we even knew we needed forgiveness. Romans 5:8 declares, "But God shows his love for us in that while we were yet sinners Christ died for us."

It is this very love, sacrificially given to us, that finally subdues our hard hearts and motivates us to undefiled devotion. Dictators cannot win the devotion of their followers through force or fear. God wins our hearts by humbling us with the magnitude of His love. We then serve Him, not to earn His love, but because we are already loved (1 John 4:19).

Cultivate a Desire for God

Undefiled devotion to Jesus creates within our hearts a hunger for more of God. We yearn to know Him more, to be with Him, to be in His presence. As the hymn writer declared, "Beyond the sacred page we seek Thee, Lord." It was this desire, placed in my heart by the Lord, that led me to ask my family to rearrange our priorities concerning the telephone, TV, and stereo. These wonderful modern conveniences had begun to destroy our desire to spend time with Jesus. The voices of musicians and game-show hosts were so loud that we could not hear the still, small voice of the Lord.

God created us to be beings of desire and passion. The ability to feel, to yearn, and to desire is God given. Habits of the heart are developed as we cultivate these passions and feed them with the object of our desire. Long ago I heard a friend say, "You plant a thought and reap a choice; plant a choice and reap a habit; plant a habit and reap character; plant character and reap a destiny."

It is God's will that we cultivate the passions of our heart for godliness and holiness. The process begins in the mind, not the emotions. The emotions will follow what the mind dwells upon. The Scriptures teach us to think righteous thoughts. Paul wrote, "To be carnally minded is death, but to be spiritually minded is life and peace" (Romans 8:6, NKJV). The great apostle also spoke of his personal desire to focus his mind on Christ in order to "know him and the power of his resurrection" (Philippians 3:10). The psalmist declared, "As the deer pants for streams of water, so my soul pants for you, O God. My soul thirsts for God, for the living God" (Psalm 42:1,2, NIV).

Some people find it very difficult to think in terms of "loving" Jesus or to speak of desire for Jesus in intimate and personal terms. Jerry Bridges comments on this difficulty:

Perhaps this idea of a desire for God sounds strange to many Christians today. We understand the thought of serving God, of being busy in his work. We may even have a "quiet time" when we read the Bible and pray. But the idea of a longing for God himself, of wanting to deeply enjoy his fellowship and his presence, may seem a bit too mystical, almost bordering on fanaticism. We prefer our Christianity to be more practical.... Yet who could be more practical than Paul? Who was more involved in the struggles of daily living than David? Still, with all their responsibilities, both Paul and David yearned to experience more fellowship with the Living God.[2]

Though we live in a complex world, devotion to the Lord Jesus is a simple matter—not necessarily easy, but simple. By turning off the TV, by tuning out worldly music, by shutting down the telephone and turning away from some activities that were pressed upon us as a family, we were able to cultivate our desire for God. Devotion to Jesus simply requires giving our hearts totally to Him.

But sometimes that simple commitment leads to an all out war with Satan. The spirit of the age is a satanic spirit. The devil will do everything he can to keep us from loving Jesus. Until we recognize Satan's involvement and overcome it, we will not be holy and acceptable to the Lord.

—14—
The Greatest Hindrance to Holiness

I 'm grateful for books warning us against cults and New Age thinking, but I haven't noticed many bestsellers about how to overcome pride, lust, or covetousness, have you? I sometimes wonder why so much is written and spoken today about protecting the church from false prophets who threaten from without while so little warning is issued about the greater danger to holiness which resides in the heart. To be sure, I need help from my brothers and sisters in the body of Christ to maintain sound doctrine in light of the false teaching which abounds today. But I need a lot more help living out the doctrine of holiness I already understand but so often fail to obey.

The greatest threat to the church today is not the seduction of our doctrine by false teaching, but the seduction of our hearts and minds by the spirit of the age. James wrote, "What causes wars, and what causes fightings among you? Is it not your passions that are at war in your members?" (James 4:1). And pride is at the center of it all.

133

Pride is our most dangerous enemy. Pride is the greatest hindrance to holiness. It is the unseen sin whose effects are found everywhere. It is the chief cause of human strife and tragedy. It is the source to which all other forms of sin can be traced. It is the sin that led to Adam and Eve's expulsion from the garden. Ignored and undealt with, pride wreaks havoc in the lives of every person on this planet.

Pride is no respecter of persons. Its victims are old and young, rich and poor, ordained ministers and laypeople. And it camouflages itself in many subtle ways. The spirit of the age gains entrance to our heart through the doorway of pride. By depending on money, technology, and comfort instead of God, we are asserting a prideful authority over our lives. We are saying by our actions that we are better prepared to rule over our lives than God is. Dependence on the idols of this world is an act of presumption. At the root of presumption is the hidden sin of pride.

Pride is not only a problem for the powerful, the famous, and the successful. Those of us who have struggled with insecurities and fears also know how pride can block our healing and deliverance. I struggled for years with painful feelings of inadequacy. At college, I was captain of the basketball team and president of the student body, but inside I was driven by feelings of insecurity. I couldn't admit to myself or others how lonely and self-conscious I was.

Years later, when a man of God prayed for me and exposed my pride through his prayer, I finally understood how pride had held me prisoner for so long. He prayed something like this: "Lord, help my friend Floyd. You see his insecurities, Lord Jesus, and how hard it is for him to acknowledge how he feels inside. Help him open up to you and others and admit he is hurting and needs help. Heal him, and set him free from this terrible sense of inadequacy and self-consciousness."

As he prayed I began to weep. His prayer touched something very deep within me. I was conscious that my hidden fears were being revealed to everyone in that prayer meeting through that man's prayer. But I didn't care; I wanted to be like Jesus. I could have resisted my friend's prayer and resented him for praying so honestly. But that would have been another exercise in pride. I wanted to be free from pride. I wanted to be closer to Jesus. I didn't want to go my own way any longer. I quietly made a choice to embrace the answer to my friend's prayer no matter what others thought of me.

Going Our Own Way

What is pride? We talk about being proud of our achievements and abilities, proud of our spouse, and proud of our children. But this is not the destructive kind of pride the Bible talks about. Indeed, the Bible admonishes us to have an honest estimation of the abilities and strengths of ourselves and our loved ones. That's a positive brand of pride.

Rather, the kind of pride the Bible condemns is an undue sense of our own superiority and an inflated level of self-esteem. Pride is an unwillingness to see ourselves as we really are, especially when we are rebellious or hurt. Pride is extreme self-centeredness. Pride is pretending to be something we're not. Pride is refusing to acknowledge our weaknesses. Pride is hiding our sin and insecurities from the very people with whom we should be open. Pride is hiding behind excuses, rationalizations, and defense mechanisms.

I was painfully proud as a child. I didn't consciously choose to be a proud person. I just didn't know how to open up about my hurts. I hadn't been taught about the freedom that comes from simply acknowledging our disappointments and insecurities, and striving to be accepted. So I covered up my inner struggle by overachieving in sports and student activities. I was too proud to admit that I felt insecure. I needed God to help me break out of the prison pride had built around my heart.

Pride is our greatest obstacle to loving and serving others. It is the greatest barrier to getting free from the grip of self-centeredness. It is the reason we have pushed God to the sidelines of our lives. We honor Him with public prayers, but we reject him as the Lord of life. Left undealt with, pride will eventually deceive us and blind us to its working in our lives. The prophet Obadiah wrote, "The pride of your heart has deceived you" (Obediah 1:3).

Pride is so subtle. The devil doesn't walk up and announce he is going to attack us with pride. Pride doesn't suddenly overtake us like uncontrollable lust. No, pride is more insidious and treacherous than that. It comes silently and often imperceptibly at first, working its poison into our hearts.

In his book *Mere Christianity*, C.S. Lewis says about pride:

> It is pride that has been the chief cause of misery in every nation and family since the world began. Other vices may sometimes bring people together. You may find good fellowship, jokes, and friendliness amongst drunken people or unchaste people, but pride always means enmity. It is enmity not only between man and man, but between man and God. In God you come up against something that is in every respect immeasurably superior to yourself. Unless you know God as that and therefore know yourself as nothing in comparison, you do not know God at all. As long as you are proud, you cannot know God. A proud man is always looking down on things and people. Of course, as long as you are looking down, you cannot see something that is

above you. You will never be able to know God as long as you are proud.[1]

Jesus had to deal with pride in His disciples. James and John had things all worked out. When they got to heaven, one was going sit on Jesus' right side, the other on His left. All they needed to bring this about was for Jesus to use His "influence" and arrange things with His Father. Instead of cooperating with their prideful plans, however, Jesus gave James and John a lesson on servanthood (Mark 10:35-45).

We often idealize the early Christians as saintly and humble. But the writers of the Epistles had to remind many of the New Testament churches of their potential for pride, as Paul did in Galatians 5:26: "Let us not become boastful, challenging one another, envying one another" (NASB).

Throughout the history of the church pride has continued to poison local congregations with bitterness, division, and strife. Pride causes us to judge others, categorizing them as inferior to us in some way. If you consider someone inferior to you, your relationship with that person will reflect your pride. Instead of loving and serving that person, you will scorn and castigate him at every opportunity and feel justified in doing so. Thus pride cripples our ability to get along with others and leaves us isolated and alone. Pride tears apart relationships between husband and wife, parent and child, and leaves hurt, bitterness, and alienation in the place of love and trust. The tragic state of the American family today is the legacy of pride at work.

Furthermore, pride in Christians also divides churches. These Christians murmur against the pastor and malign the elders. They judge their fellow believers and promote division and dissension. In the end they alienate and divide the body of Christ which, through love and unity, is supposed to be a reflection of God to society at large.

The Source of Pride

The Bible declares that Satan is the author of pride. In Isaiah's allegorical narrative, Satan boasts, "I will ascend to heaven; I will raise my throne above the stars of God, and I will sit on the mount of assembly in the recesses of the north. I will ascend above the heights of the clouds; I will make myself like the Most High" (Isaiah 14:13,14, NASB).

Satan's entire emphasis is on what he thinks he can do. His last claim is perhaps his most revealing. He believes he has the ability to make himself like God. Notice how many times the word *I* occurs in the passage. Satan scorned dependence upon God and chose his own wisdom and way of doing things.

Throughout the millennia of human history these same self-exalting thoughts have echoed over and over through human hearts. Each of us at some time has repeated them in our heart. We continue to believe we can do things without God. We think we can take God's place and steer our life in any direction we choose.

Satan uses pride to try to paralyze our efforts to acknowledge God and thus alienate us from God. "Surely," we rationalize, "a little pride won't hurt us." The Bible makes no such concession to pride. God is merciful, but the Bible straightforwardly teaches that God refuses to answer the proud person (Job 35:12). Pride is an abomination to the Lord (Proverbs 16:5,18), and He will not tolerate it. Indeed, as James 4:6 tells us, God goes out of His way to resist and oppose the proud.

But we need God on our side. We need His strength and wisdom in our lives. We need His grace and redeeming power. It is foolish, therefore, to alienate ourselves from God through pride. Proverbs 26:12 tells us there is only one thing worse than a fool: a person who is "wise in his own eyes." And why is a proud person a bigger fool than a fool?

Because his pride leads to his ultimate destruction. We desperately need God, and to alienate ourselves from Him through pride is the most foolish and self-destructive thing we can ever possibly do.

The Symptoms of Pride

Pride is like cancer. At first you're unaware of it as it grows undetected inside your body. Gradually you become aware that something isn't functioning as it should. You detect aches and pains, you feel nauseated, a discoloration or growth appears. Now you're faced with two choices: go to a doctor for diagnosis and treatment or pretend nothing is wrong. In the early stages of cancer you can hide the symptoms and pretend nothing's wrong. But as time goes by the problem becomes more difficult to conceal. The once small, seemingly insignificant growth has become a consuming and terminal illness.

So it is with pride. At first the symptoms are almost unnoticeable. You become a little impatient when inconvenienced. You avoid certain people. It takes you a little longer to forgive someone who offends you. You struggle to say "You're right and I'm wrong" when corrected.

As I have thought about how pride developed in my own life, I have been able to identify some of its symptoms. Perhaps the following symptoms from my own experience will help you identify the presence of pride in your life which, left undealt with, will keep you from walking in holiness.

Taking Credit for What God Has Done

This is a dangerous form of pride that provokes us to take the credit for what we have done for the Lord or for the gifts the Lord has given us. We tend to tell stories of how God used us to witness to someone or help someone in such a way that others see us in better light. But we can do nothing apart from God. By giving the impression that we are in some way responsible for these gifts, we take the credit away from Him when He emphatically states, "I will not give My glory to another" (Isaiah 42:8, NASB).

A Demanding Spirit

The pride of a demanding person's heart is revealed by constantly bringing attention to what has *not* been done for him rather than to what *has* been done for him. In demanding that people do things our way, we are in essence saying, "I am superior to you."

Superiority

Pride can cause us to feel we are more important than others and to look down on them. We act haughtily and in a manner revealing an attitude of condescension, a belief that somehow we are closer to God or just better than other people because of our doctrines, actions, or intrinsic worth.

Sarcasm

Caustic comments may be socially acceptable, but they have no place in the kingdom of God. Sarcasm is a thinly veiled attempt to impress people by highlighting the faults of others in a pseudohumorous way. It is always at the expense of another person and reveals the prejudice of our heart.

A Judgmental and Critical Attitude

Criticism divides and destroys the church. Jesus died to make us one. Proud people are critical and judgmental, and have difficulty seeing the good in others. When they do see the good in others they are quick to negate it through their critical approach.

Impatience

Impatience signifies that our ideas, projects, programs, and schedules are more important than people. When our agenda does not go as planned we express our lack of love and self-control through impatience.

Envy and Greed

Envy and greed stem from the basic belief that we have a right to possess more than we presently have. Greed is an attitude which views the world on the basis of what we want instead of what we already have. Envy is the same attitude, only it's directed specifically at wanting what someone else has. Envy and greed infect our spirit and rob us of our hunger for spiritual reality.

Hardness of Heart

As Christians we are called to "rejoice with those who rejoice, weep with those who weep" (Romans 12:15). Hardhearted people more often find themselves secretly rejoicing when things don't go well for others. They are aloof and unable to comfort and encourage others or rejoice with them in their blessings. They cannot express affection or tenderness.

An Unteachable Spirit

None of us is above the need for instruction or correction. When confronted by someone on an issue, do we listen to them or ignore what they have to say? Do we accept their reproof or become aloof and resentful that someone would dare correct us? Unteachableness is a symptom of pride.

Disloyalty and Unforgiveness

Pride tries to excuse disloyalty by whispering to us, "You've been hurt, you have a right to get even." Nursing hurt feelings is not an option for Christians. We are never justified in criticizing or turning against others. As the old adage says, "Two wrongs don't make a right."

People-Pleasing

By trying to please people and live up to their expectations for us, we can easily fall into a form of false spirituality. We find ourselves praying, reading Scripture, and worshiping, not from the heart, but from a desire to impress others with our spirituality. We become more interested in how we look to others than in how we look to the Lord. The more insecure we are, the more susceptible we become to the opinions of others.

Flattery

Flattery is a form of manipulation. It is an insincere attempt to win another person's favor. Flattery is often used as bait. It is dangled before people to probe their loyalties and vulnerabilities. If the bait is taken, the flatterer knows he has found a person whose weaknesses he can exploit.

Self-Pity

Self-pity is the direct result of being too proud to turn our problems over to the Lord, choosing rather to cling to our hurts, frustrations, and disappointments.

Dealing with the Root Cause

You have two choices when you discover the symptoms of pride in your life. You can either ignore the symptoms as insignificant, or go to God and ask Him to reveal the pride in your heart and help you deal with it. If you cover the symptoms instead of responding to them, your pride will not go away. It will continue to grow and fester unchecked in your heart until it consumes you and destroys you.

Even when we deal with pride the way we should, we will never be completely free of its influence. It is always a snare for the unwary. However, we can avoid its hold on us.

Often I have needed the help of others in recognizing areas of pride in my life. It's not easy to have pride revealed to us. When faced with the truth about ourselves from others, it is not always easy to admit our failure. But if we are to rid ourselves of pride we must be willing to learn the truth about ourselves no matter how horrible it may seem.

God's intention in revealing pride in our lives is always for our benefit. He wants to help us, not humiliate us. Through generation after generation God, with great sadness of heart, has watched the destruction and hurt pride has wrought in His people. He longs for us to be free of pride's hold over us. We must take the crucial step of asking Him to reveal the pride in our hearts. God longs for us to be holy, but it can't happen if we are proud.

When He reveals your pride, either directly to your heart or through the loving confrontation of others, you must act. You must set the ax to the root of pride and remove it from your heart. If you are to walk in holiness you can do no less. Holiness cannot flourish in a life where pride abounds.

The spirit of the age is rooted in pride. It pushes self to the fore. It is interested only in self-gratification. It has created an immoral world where pride reigns unchecked.

Such an environment is hostile to the notion of holiness. Holiness condemns the spirit of the age. It declares to pride, "I live by a different standard. You have no hold over me. You are defeated." Holiness shines a light of hope into our dark and fallen world. It says, "You don't have to live like that. There is a better way. There is hope. You can be set free from the bondage of pride."

To attain holiness, pride must be radically dealt with. The easiest way to deal with pride is to let its opposite— brokenness and humility—take root and grow in our hearts. Nurtured and tended, these qualities of godliness will grow and displace pride. We'll look more closely at these positive qualities in the next chapter.

— 15 —
The Practice of Humility

S ince pride is the greatest obstacle to holiness in our lives as believers, the primary quality needed to encourage holiness is humility. Yet this important characteristic is shunned in a society committed to self-fulfillment, achievement, and advancement. The idea of humility is shrugged off as something for sniveling, weak-kneed wimps or for people like Mother Teresa and Billy Graham. Missionaries and pastors pursue humility, but not "ordinary" Christians. "I just don't have the time for that sort of thing," we rationalize. We're too busy modeling ourselves after the so-called heroes of the age: the rich, the famous, business tycoons, gods and goddesses of beauty.

The spirit of the age will keep us from seeking and knowing God. Pride must be replaced by personal broken-ness and humility, which is the cornerstone of holiness. Holiness can never develop in the life of a proud person. If you want to be a holy man or woman of God, you must become a humble man or woman. Holiness and humility are inseparable. You can't have one without the other.

The Word on Humility

There are many misconceptions about humility among believers. What is it really? Humility is first and foremost dependence upon God. It is God's human creation acknowledging its absolute and total dependence upon the Creator. Humble men and women look to God daily as their friend and only source of forgiveness and mercy.

Humility is a longing in the heart for relationship and communion with God. Humility drives us past mere religion to a growing personal relationship with the living God.

Humility releases us from hiding and pretending to be something we are not. It allows us to be known for who we really are. A world concerned with superficiality encourages us to cover our weaknesses. Humility sets us free from this kind of thinking. Straightforward admission to others of our needs and shortcomings allows us to be free from the deceit of pride.

The Bible is specific regarding humility's importance to believers. Jesus said, "Whoever humbles himself like this child, he is the greatest in the kingdom of heaven" (Matthew 18:4). The psalmist declared, "The Lord takes pleasure in his people; he adorns the humble with victory" (Psalm 149:4). Solomon wrote, "Toward the scorners he is scornful, but to the humble he shows favor" (Proverbs 3:34). Job said, "For God abases the proud, but he saves the lowly" (Job 22:29). James echoes, "God opposes the proud, but gives grace to the humble" (James 4:6). Peter and James both instructed the early Christians with the words, "Humble yourselves" (1 Peter 5:6; James 4:10).

Paul made it clear in his writings that humility will affect every area of our lives. To first-century believers he wrote, "Honor one another above yourselves" (Romans 12:10, NIV); "If anyone thinks he is something, when he is nothing, he deceives himself" (Galatians 6:3); "Be completely humble and gentle; be patient, bearing with one another in love. Make every effort to keep the unity of the Spirit" (Ephesians 4:2,3, NIV); "Do nothing out of selfish ambition or vain conceit, but in humility consider others better than yourselves. Each of you should look not only to your own interests, but also to the interests of others" (Philippians 2:3,4, NIV); "As God's chosen people, holy and dearly beloved, clothe yourselves with compassion, kindness, humility, gentleness and patience. Bear with each other and forgive whatever grievances you may have against one another. Forgive as the Lord forgave you" (Colossians 3:12-14).

Humility in Action

How does humility work its way out in practical daily living for Christians? Let me share with you several specific ways biblical humility will exercise itself in opposition to the spirit of the age.

Humble Christians Focus on the Lord

The person who stands at the center of your life holds the key to your spiritual growth. In comparing the carnal and the spiritual man in Romans 7 and 8, Paul focuses on the relative self-centeredness of each. The carnal man is preoccupied with himself. He is the center of his own universe. The word I is used 25 times in these two chapters to describe the carnal man. By contrast, I is used only twice in the description of the spiritual man. We can have only one life-focus at a time. Either we are focusing on the Lord or we are living supremely for ourselves.

Pride focuses on self. Pride holds us prisoner to self-righteousness, self-pity, self-sufficiency, self-congratulation, and self-indulgence.

Humility focuses on the Lord. Choosing to focus on the Lord frees us from the wretched state of preoccupation with self to enjoy God and others in a way a proud person cannot.

Humble Christians Serve Others

One of the great paradoxes of Christianity involves humility. The person who wants to be great in the kingdom of God must be humble to be the servant of all (Matthew 20:26,27). Jesus, our great example, "emptied himself, taking the form of a servant" (Philippians 2:7). The people who serve the most in the kingdom are those who understand that Jesus became a bondservant to them. With this revelation our primary motivation in the Christian life is serving as we have been served.

Nothing more clearly reveals the motives of the heart than how we react when asked to serve others. Do we consider certain tasks, such as contact with the poor, below our dignity? Do we think we're too good to touch the homeless? Are we too important to help with the lowliest of jobs?

Humble Christians Learn from Others

Pride gives us a very narrow perspective on life. We believe we have all the right answers, so we do not recognize our need to learn from others. Humility, by contrast, realizes that there are things of value to be learned from everyone.

We need humility's broader perspective. That doesn't mean we should be tossed to and fro by everything we are told. It does mean, however, that we recognize our need of other believers. We need the spiritual and doctrinal balance and protection they bring to us. None of us possesses all the answers to the problems of life. Could it be that God does not give a full revelation of truth to any one individual or group in order to keep us dependent on each other?

Humble Christians Encourage Others

Giving encouragement is an easy and painless way to develop humility. It changes our perspective on other people because we must get to know them if we are going to encourage them. To recognize their strengths and positive qualities we must get close to them. Pride holds us back from encouraging others, wanting us to focus on a person's sins and weaknesses. Encouraging others is a joyous experience for a humble person.

Humble Christians Trust Others

God has given us the most precious gift of all: His love and trust. Are we worthy of that trust? No, of course not. Yet He continues to trust us. Do we extend to others that same trust?

Trusting anyone in a sinful world is risky business. Yet God thought it was a risk worth taking with us. He does not trust us because we are perfect, but because of His mercy. His trust is not based on our performance. In the same manner we must make grace the basis of the trust we place in others.

Humble Christians Lay Down Their Rights

Society's prevailing mentality toward rights seems to be, "If I don't watch out for my rights, nobody else will." But Christians march to the beat of a different drummer. Jesus is our example when it comes to personal rights. He was accused, maligned, and betrayed, yet He did not fight for His rights. He forgave those who accused Him, blessed those who persecuted Him, and willingly laid down His life for all mankind. Are you prepared to give up your rights? Only through humility can we do so.

Humble Christians Seek Justice for Others

People not only sin, they are also sinned against. Proverbs 31:8,9 tells us that God's people are to defend the rights of those who are sinned against: the poor and downtrodden of society. The gospel must be applied to social injustices if we are to take it seriously.

We may be misunderstood for defending the poor and homeless. But if we stand by silently in the face of injustice and inequality, we have given in to the spirit of the age. Humble followers of Christ lay aside public opinion and speak for those who have no voice.

Humble Christians Confess Their Needs and Weaknesses to Others

Ironically, the key to victory in the Christian life is found in learning how to handle failure. Christ's power is made perfect in weakness. If we say we are not weak, we have no need of His power. Conversely, when we acknowledge our limitations and weaknesses, we are free to ask the Lord and others for their help.

A proud person covers his weaknesses, but a humble person admits them. Covering up deep-seated fears is a form of pride that keeps others from reaching out to help us. Humility frees us from the fear of failure and allows us to embrace the love and affirmation of others—which we all need. Admitting our weaknesses, especially our feelings of inferiority, is one of the surest ways to overcome pride.

Humility, along with its expressions, is not something God does to us. Rather, the attitude and actions of humility are our responsibility. "Humble yourselves," James wrote to believers (James 4:6). Humbling ourselves doesn't mean that we wait for some feeling of worthlessness to come over us. It doesn't mean that we wear threadbare or unattractive clothes. Humility is not achieved by using self-degrading Christian clichés in our prayers or by praying with a vocal tremor or tone that supposedly indicates greater spirituality. Humility is a heart attitude and daily response to people that we are responsible to maintain.

Humility in This Age

It is said that Martin Luther was once asked to name the three greatest Christian virtues. He replied, "Humility, humility, and humility." Humility is an imperative for today's Christians. If we want to see the church revived and society impacted for God, we must be willing to say no to the pride which characterizes society. We must practice humility. The world does not want to see a procession of proud and deceitful people who call themselves Christians. It wants to see changed people, people who live out what they say they believe. Changed people bring hope to an otherwise hopeless society. We must change and live by the standard of the Spirit instead of the standard of the world. Humility is the soil in which all other fruits of the Spirit grow.

Proud religious acts performed for God may satisfy the soul for a period of time. But there comes a moment when the dry ground of one's spirit cries out for more than it has experienced before. Our tendency is to substitute form for reality, action for relationship, and busyness for communion. Humility cries out for reality. Humility says that we must no longer substitute doing for being or religious fervor for spiritual reality. We must know our Creator and Lord personally and intimately.

In an age of flashy, aggressive, name-it-and-claim-it Christianity, there is a great danger that we may neglect the difficult but crucial process of building a foundation of godly character in our lives. Humility is not always a popular virtue, nor is it always understood. To some it appears to be weakness, cowardice, a lack of boldness, or even a lack of faith. But to those who pay the price, there is no regret.

In my book *Wholehearted* (InterVarsity Press), I described a crisis point in my relationship with others. I had hurt several close friends deeply, showed disrespect for my wife, and was being dealt with by God in many areas of my relationship with Him. I went for a walk one day in the forest near our home. I decided to put my life totally on the line to the Lord. I knew at that point it had to be all or nothing. No superficial response could deal with the crisis I had created for myself.

I humbled myself and confessed my predicament to the Lord, acknowledging my sin. Then I prayed a prayer something like this:

> Lord, I desperately need You in my life. I have come to the end of myself. I choose not to go around this situation. I ask You to use this time in my life to bring me to a place of brokenness. Do anything You need to do to produce humility and Christlikeness in me.
>
> I ask You to be ruthless in dealing with my sin. No matter how long it takes, Lord, or what You have to do, I welcome Your loving judgment in my heart. Expose anything and everything in my life You want to deal with.
>
> No matter what the cost, Lord, I commit myself to Your way. I refuse to push myself forward or to avoid Your dealings in my character. I ask for no short cuts to my growth. If it takes 10, 15, or 20 years, I say yes to You, Lord.

It was at my point of humility that God really began to work in my character. I invited Him to refine me with fire, no matter how hot it got! I asked for His bright light of truth to flood my heart, no matter what it revealed. I asked God to produce brokenness and godliness in me, no matter how long it took. I decided to believe that God wanted to use every conflict I had with people from that point on to show me what was in my heart.

The vital importance of humility is reflected in the words of L.E. Maxwell written many years ago:

> Many people wonder why they have no victory over their wounded pride, their touchiness, their greediness.... The secret is not far away. They secretly and habitually practice shrine worship—at the shrine of self. In the outward cross they glory, but inwardly they worship another god and stretch out their hands to serve a pitied, petty, and pampered self-life. Until Christ works out in you an inner crucifixion which will cut you off from self-infatuation and unite you to God in a deep union of love, a thousand heavens could not give you peace.[1]

I ask you today to humble yourself as this passage suggests and make the same commitment I made years ago, a commitment I still hold with all my heart. I cannot express to you how glad I am that I have chosen God's way. God has been faithful to me, and I rejoice that He has answered my prayer!

— 16 —
Opening Our Lives to Others

T he Bible is a record of God's dealings with people, both individuals and groups. God is interested in each of us as individuals, but He has a special interest in people living in community. As far back as Genesis 2 we find God evaluating an individual alone. Everything was perfect in the Garden of Eden. The flowers were blooming, the streams were sparkling as they tumbled along, and the crops were growing. What more could Adam need?

But seeing Adam alone with only plants and animals for companionship, God said, "It is not good that man should be alone" (v. 18). God saw that a basic need in Adam was going unmet. Adam needed "a helper fit for him," a partner in life. So God created Eve for Adam, and God has been putting people together in families, churches, communities, and tribes ever since.

The Old Testament is the saga of covenant relationships between God and people. We read repeatedly that God is the God of Abraham, Isaac, and Jacob. The many genealogies listed in the Old Testament reveal that being linked to past and future generations was important to the Jewish sense of national identity. God was interested in perpetuating a closely knit group of people which bore His name.

The New Testament perpetuates the concept of God's interest in people together. The bulk of the four Gospels are about Jesus calling and training the 12 disciples. Have you ever thought about the way in which Jesus trained the disciples? He could easily have called each of them one by one at four-month intervals and given them one-on-one instruction. After all, isn't individual instruction the most effective form of teaching? Perhaps it is if you want to learn theory. But if you want practical experience in Christian living, discipleship must include other people. The lessons the disciples had to learn could not be learned in a vacuum.

The Book of Acts is the record of God working through His church as expressed in house groups. Think for a moment about some of the names given to the New Testament church: the family of God, one body, the household of the faithful, the fellowship of believers, the Bride of Christ, saints together. These are corporate names, names which denote oneness of purpose and fellowship.

In each of his letters to the churches, Paul wrote of God's dealings with His people and tells us that relationship is the essence of His covenant with people. The Bible is about people in relationship with one another: people loving each other, hurting each other, deceiving each other, forgiving each other, comforting each other, and interacting with each other as God strives to mold them into His image.

The spirit of the age expresses itself in individualism—a go-it-alone way of life. It fosters the attitude, "I don't need you, and you don't need me," which stands in stark contrast to God's purpose in creating us for relationship. Satan knows God's purpose, so he fights against true

Christianity by promoting loneliness and isolation every way he can. We defeat the spirit of the age by cooperating with God's plan of being involved in relationship with each other, especially as believers.

Being Holy Together

What is the purpose of fellowship with other believers and why is it so important? Holiness in a modern world is not an individual affair. The isolation and privatization of believers makes holiness impossible. Individualistic Christianity is a contradiction of terms. We cannot stand alone. Participation in a community of believers held together by close relationships makes it possible for us to be set apart from the world.

Christian fellowship provides a place of refuge from the world, a place where we can freely and frankly assess ourselves and our relationship to Christ. It is a place where we are accepted. It is a place where we can find help in trouble. To be a genuine Christian is to be part of a community of close-knit brothers and sisters.

What sets this community apart from the spirit of the age? What are the biblical characteristics of a caring fellowship? There are a number of critical traits which should identify your relationship with other believers.

Worshiping with One Another

Paul wrote, "Let the word of Christ dwell in you richly, as you teach and admonish one another in all wisdom, and as you sing psalms and hymns and spiritual songs with thankfulness in your hearts to God" (Colossians 3:16). The act of worship has its greatest fulfillment when the people of God bring their gifts of adoration *together* before the Lord. Yes, individuals can and should worship God in the privacy of personal devotions. But the corporate nature of true Christianity is realized in believers worshiping together.

Corporate worship captures the essence of God's purpose for creating people who love each other and live for His glory. When we worship together we are clearly demonstrating our love for God and for each other in the same activity.

Encouraging One Another

The New Testament admonishes us to be encouragers: "Let us consider how to stir up one another to love and good works, not neglecting to meet together, as is the habit of some, but encouraging one another, and all the more as you see the Day drawing near" (Hebrews 10:24); "Therefore encourage one another and build one another up, just as you are doing" (1 Thessalonians 5:11). Is there anyone who doesn't feel the need to be encouraged? No, of course not. We need to know that other believers recognize our efforts and see progress in our lives.

But how do we go about encouraging others? What difficulties are our fellow believers trying to overcome? In what areas are they weary? What are their felt needs? Good questions, but how do we find the answers? There is one important way to answer these questions: We must get to know people! If we are to encourage each other in deepening and applying our faith we must know who "each other" is and the problems we each face. After all, the areas in which we need the most encouragement are those areas where we feel the least adequate and confident, and we usually conceal those areas from each other.

We must take encouragement one step at a time. Don't rush up to an unsuspecting person and pry their problems out of them. Trust must be earned. Start slowly. I believe this is one of the main reasons hospitality is so greatly emphasized in Paul's writings. As we open our hearts and homes to each other, trust, sharing of real needs, and encouragement follow.

Sharing One Another's Burdens

The importance of mutual burden-bearing is clear in Scripture: "Bear one another's burdens, and so fulfill the law of Christ" (Galatians 6:2); "Rejoice with those who rejoice, weep with those who weep" (Romans 12:15). But before people will allow you to know their intimate needs, relationships must be built. This takes time and effort. Holiness in a busy world means resisting the spirit of individualism. It means taking time to get involved with others at church. As we revamp our values and priorities to include people, relationships have an opportunity to grow. We have the time to listen and care.

How different our churches would be if each of us committed ourselves to never hearing another person's problems without doing something about them. I'm not saying that we can always put things right for others. Sometimes all we can do is to listen, but that is often what is needed the most.

Correcting One Another

Confronting and correcting one another is a biblical discipline: "If a man is overtaken by any trespass, you who are spiritual should restore him in a spirit of gentleness" (Galatians 6:1); "Faithful are the wounds of a friend" (Proverbs 27:6); "Iron sharpens iron, and one man sharpens another" (Proverbs 27:17). Investing time in building relationships allows us to see one another's deep needs and hidden faults. Eyeing one another critically from ten rows away in church on Sunday morning does not lay the foundation for loving correction. But close friendship does. If we love our friends, we will speak up when we see them trapped in error. Love cannot be silent when sin is present. Correction does not mean condemning; it means caring enough to gently confront.

Being Accountable to One Another

There is no word that frightens Christians today like the word "accountability." We have so privatized our marriages, our businesses, our families, and the use of our time that the very thought of being accountable to others is foreign to our thinking.

Yet the instruction of Scripture is clear: "Therefore, putting away falsehood, let every one speak the truth with his neighbor, for we are members of one another" (Ephesians 4:25); "Be subject to one another out of reverence for Christ" (Ephesians 5:21). Paul tells us we are to speak the truth and submit to one another in the church. What do these statements really mean? Are we to be totally subjected to our leaders like the devotees of a cult? Are we to have every detail of our lives scrutinized by others?

There are two meanings of the word "submit." The first meaning is for one person to accept the control or superior strength of another. The second meaning is for one person to allow the plans of others to be considered and any flaws in them illuminated. The latter meaning is the pattern for accountability between Christian brothers and sisters.

Practically speaking, how do we do this? Cultivate a small, close group of Christians with whom you develop a level of trust in order to freely share your thoughts, feelings, plans, sins, and frustrations. The group can be as few as two or as many as 20-25. It is important that group members be committed to listen to one another, pray for one another, and share godly advice with one another and receive these ministries from one another in return.

Unlike the "doormat" concept of submission, biblical submission calls us to be accountable to one another for our actions, although ultimately the course we each take in life is our own responsibility. Submission does not mean absolute obedience. Obedience is given to God; submission is given to another person. In being open and accountable to others for wisdom and insights we reduce the risk of making major mistakes. More importantly, we overcome the independent spirit of the age by living a holy life.

Sharing Material Wealth with One Another

The New Testament Epistles strongly emphasize that we give our material wealth to other believers in need: "If anyone has the world's goods and sees his brother in need, yet closes his heart against him, how does God's love abide in him?" (1 John 3:17); "Do not neglect to do good and to share what you have, for such sacrifices are pleasing to God" (Hebrews 13:16); "For you were called to freedom, brethren; only do not use your freedom as an opportunity for the flesh, but through love be servants of one another" (Galatians 5:13).

Perhaps you don't know one single Christian in need. In that case I hope you are challenged to get out of your personal "comfort zone"! There are brothers and sisters everywhere who are in need of our caring gifts. Get to know people, take time to get involved, and you will learn about the people in your church who have material needs.

Once we are aware of people with needs, how do we give them our gifts? The Bible tells us to do so without fanfare or desire for recognition (Matthew 6:1-4). Instead, give your gift anonymously through others or slip it secretly into the needy person's pocket, purse, or Bible. The joy of giving far outlasts whatever joy you may receive spending that money on yourself. If you are a professional person or have a marketable skill, give your time and talent to those who cannot afford your services.

When Community Is Lacking

Sadly, these biblical characteristics are being slowly eroded in a culture heavily influenced by the spirit of the age. We have lost the sense of community God designed for our mutual support and encouragement. Instead of a nurturing fellowship, the church has become a Hollywood production: big business, well-run programs, and entertainment.

We have turned the church into a spectator sport. We sit on comfortable pews around the outside of the arena staring at the backs of each other's heads while the song leader, the choir, and the pastor perform for us. Then we shuffle past the pastor, shake his hand, and head off to Sunday dinner. As we leave we evaluate the service on a scale of one to ten as if it were a competitive event. "Well, I gave the choir a score of five; the altos were flat. But the pastor's sermon was a minus two. What a drag! He told the same old stories again." Sometimes we get more support out of a Rotary Club meeting or shopping with friends than we do from church.

If this is your experience in your church, take heart. At least you have caught a glimpse of what more it could be. Your church should be a united, caring community in which all members are being encouraged and enabled toward holiness. But if it isn't, don't despair. There are some positive steps you can take.

First, be patient. Remember: Your convictions were not shaped in a day. You may be seeing for the first time how valuable a functioning community can be. Allow others time to discover this truth.

The human tendency is to leave your church and try to find a "perfect" church. Don't start looking! I have traveled extensively and spoken to thousands of church leaders and lay people. Believe me: There is no perfect church this side of heaven! Even if you happen to find a perfect church, don't join it—you'll spoil it! Unless God clearly leads otherwise, stay where you are. Allow God to use you as a catalyst to bring others into a deeper awareness of their importance to each other.

Second, take the initiative to change yourself, not to sit in judgment of others. What can you do to make the church a more encouraging, loving place, a place where people will feel the love of Christ? Don't wait for others, do something! Ask God to guide you into areas which will impact those around you.

Third, pray. And when you are finished praying, pray some more. Pray until you see your church through God's eyes. He loves His church. He died for His church; it bears His name. Ask God to put His love for His church in your heart. Pray blessings down upon the church. Pray for godly leadership. Pray for revival. Pray for spiritual break-throughs. Pray against the enemy. Pray in the Spirit. Pray without ceasing. This is God's promise if we pray: "Call to Me, and I will answer you, and show you great and mighty things, which you do not know" (Jeremiah 33:3, NKJV).

Community Takes Time

It takes more than a one-hour slot of time on Sunday morning to develop a caring fellowship. It takes a lot more of the one thing none of us seems to have enough of: time. How realistic is it to think that we will actually have the time to develop all the characteristics of a nurturing fellowship in our whirlwind schedules?

We will never be delivered from the individualism which characterizes our age until we reassess the way we use our time. Our time schedules are a reflection of our priorities. When we make our plans, what values govern our priorities? Planning the day down to the last minute leaves very little room for spontaneity. When we become too structured we resent the interruptions of those in the body who need us.

When we plan our days we need to make room for prayer, Bible reading, and ministry to other people. If we don't make deliberate choices for these priorities, we will become preoccupied with ourselves and our compelling list of things to do. Paul's injunction about time is just as relevant to us as it was to the Ephesians: "Look carefully then how you walk, not as unwise men but as wise, making the most of the time, because the days are evil. Therefore do not be foolish, but understand what the will of the Lord is" (Ephesians 5:15,16).

When we evaluate our daily walk we must ask ourselves, "Am I making the most of my time? Am I using my hours and minutes wisely in light of my relationship to God and my fellow believers? Or am I living to satiate my own desires? Am I driven to perform and achieve? Is business more important to me than people? Do I have a second and even a third job in order to earn more and buy more? Have I exchanged knowing my children for giving them things? Have I traded fellowship with other believers for a one-hour slot on Sunday morning and a few bucks in the offering?"

These are hard questions, but questions which need answers. The spirit of the age attempts to seduce us away from the values of service, accountability, kindness, and compassion. Will we stand against the spirit of the age, or will we use our valuable time to pursue the almighty dollar and the easy, private lifestyle that comes with it?

Jesus gave a parable which illustrated the futility of hoarding our time and resources instead of investing them in the community of believers:

"Take heed, and beware of all covetousness; for a man's life does not consist in the abundance of his possessions." And he told them a parable, saying, "The land of the rich man brought forth plentifully; and he thought to himself, 'What shall I do, for I have nowhere to store my crops?' And he said, 'I will do this: I will pull down my barns, and build larger ones; and there I will

store all my grain and my goods. And I will say to
my soul, Soul, you have ample goods laid up for
many years; take your ease, eat, drink, be merry.'
But God said to him, 'Fool! This night your soul is
required of you; and the things you have prepared, whose will they be?' So is he who lays up
treasure for himself, and is not rich toward God"
(Luke 12:15-21).

When it comes to the use of our time and resources in
contributing to a community of believers, we must not be
swept away by the secularization, individualism, and consumerism which characterizes the spirit of the age. Instead we must obey the straightforward instructions of
James:

But be doers of the word, and not hearers only,
deceiving yourselves. For if any one is a hearer of
the word and not a doer, he is like a man who
observes his natural face in the mirror; for he
observes himself and goes away and at once forgets what he was like. But he who looks into the
perfect law, the law of liberty, and perseveres,
being no hearer that forgets but a doer that acts,
he shall be blessed in his doing (James 1:22-25).

— 17 —
Fight the Good Fight

D o you recognize, dear friend, that you are in a battle for your soul? Do you understand that Satan appeals to your selfish desires through the spirit of the age daily, trying to get you to compromise your faith in Christ? You are up against subtle spiritual powers which are intent on surrounding you and cutting you off from spiritual truth. If you do not aggressively cultivate your passion for holiness, carnal passions will take over your life. Satan will dominate you and control you. You live in a war zone every day. You cannot afford to be passive.

The Bible teaches us to resist the devil (James 4:7). If we are to overcome the spirit of the age we must take up the weapons God has provided and go on the offensive. We must fight against the spirit of the age lest we get caught up in its lies. We must battle against the spirit of the age if we are to find the time and energy necessary to cultivate a relationship with Jesus. We must resist the servant spirits of materialism, selfish individualism, pluralization, and secularization or they will render us useless to the world

God calls us to serve. Holiness, humility, and fighting the enemy go hand in hand.

We're not just battling *against* Satan and the spirit of the age; we're battling *for* our relationship with God. We're not just battling to *draw away* from Satan's influence; we're battling to *draw near* to God in holiness. James instructs us to "resist the devil" *and* "draw near to God" (James 4:7,8).

Similarly, Paul also instructed us to be aggressive when it comes to maintaining our relationship with God: "But as for you... aim at righteousness, godliness, faith, love, steadfastness, gentleness. Fight the good fight of the faith; take hold of the eternal life to which you were called" (1 Timothy 6:11,12). Notice the terms which suggest that we are in a battle: aim, fight, take hold. Holiness doesn't just happen. We must stir ourselves up to possess what is rightfully ours, the holiness which Satan is trying to steal from us every day. Spiritual warfare is the process of defeating the enemy and reclaiming what he has taken from us.

The Weapons of War

Spiritual warfare can be easily misunderstood. We're not talking about fighting people, even though some people must be resisted because of their evil influence on society. Paul reminds us that we are not contending against flesh and blood (Ephesians 6:12). Spiritual warfare is *spiritual*.

This also means that our weapons are not to be found in the external trappings of church life which are attractive to so many Christians. In fact, the strategies for holiness are so simple that many Christians look right past them. They have been fed such a steady diet of sensationalism, entertainment, and hype that they consider the true pursuit of holiness a big letdown.

No new revelation, no deeper truth, no spiritual secret, no flashy program is needed to equip you for resisting the devil and drawing near to God. Holiness and overcoming evil is achieved by plain, old-fashioned discipline—applying the simple teaching of God's changeless Word.

Paul wrote, "For though we live in the world we are not carrying on a worldly war, for the weapons of our warfare are not worldly but have divine power to destroy strongholds" (2 Corinthians 10:4,5). What are these basic weapons of war we must employ to defeat the spirit of the age and lay hold of holiness? I want to highlight several of them which are mentioned in Scripture. I urge you to pray right now that God will help you integrate this spiritual arsenal into your life to the point that you will experience the victory God has ordained for you.

Surrounded by Truth

Perhaps no spiritual weapon is as important as our love for truth. Paul said we are to clothe ourselves with truth (Ephesians 6:14). He describes the Bible, God's revelation of truth, as the "sword of the Spirit" (Ephesians 6:17). God's Word is our weapon for hand-to-hand combat with the spirit of the age.

Love for truth is the essential difference between Christians and non-Christians. Many people don't want to know the truth. We live in a dishonest, deceitful world. People will pay any price to get what they want, and that usually means compromising the truth. For example, two California researchers recently announced that 68 percent of the men and 51 percent of the women they surveyed said they would lie to a sexual partner (about marital status, previous sex partners, etc.) to get sex. This is a disturbing fact in light of the AIDS epidemic. Furthermore, 20 percent of the men surveyed said they would lie to a potential sex partner if they had already tested positive for AIDS![1] Truth in the world is a rare commodity.

We came to Jesus because He is truth personified (John 14:6). We were liberated by Jesus and set free from our self-deception by His truth (John 8:32). If we lose our love for truth, what do we have left to distinguish us from the world?

Sadly, the spirit of the age makes it is so easy for us to lie, especially to ourselves. I find it difficult to be brutally honest about my own sins and weaknesses. I am tempted to call them anything but what they are. A lie is "stretching the truth just a little bit"; stealing is "taking something that I eventually plan to return"; coveting is "admiring deeply"; lustful ogling is "just looking."

Satan is behind this compromise with truth. If he can get us to believe a lie about one sin, he will tempt us to others. We must fight the good fight for truth and against lying and dishonesty if we are to overcome the spirit of the age.

Love for truth exposes pride and self-indulgence. Love for truth liberates us from the lie that happiness comes through appeasing the flesh. Love for truth exposes the lie that materialism and consumption bring security and acceptance. Love for truth sets us free from option fatigue. Love for truth lifts us above the false good-life gospel to the life that can only be found in loving Jesus with all our heart, soul, mind, and body.

You cannot be holy if you do not love truth. Do you love truth so much that you are willing to expose every lie, every half-truth, and every sin you have covered up to get right with God and others you have sinned against? Are there relationship conflicts in your life right now because you have been unwilling to follow through on the confrontation necessary to get them right? God promises you victory if you will commit yourself to love truth.

God is the source of truth, and the Bible is the revelation of that truth. In order to love truth, you must study

God's Word regularly. Do whatever is necessary in order for you to understand it. Join a Bible class or study group. Memorize Scripture and quote it often. Attend services where the Bible is preached. And read good Bible-study books. As you saturate your mind with God's truth you will be equipped to wield the sword of the Spirit and disarm the lies of the spirit of the age.

Serving Sacrificially

Another weapon which will help us battle the spirit of the age is sacrificial service to the Lord, the kind of service that brings the gospel to people. Paul described it as "having shod your feet with the equipment of the gospel of peace" (Ephesians 6:15). To the Roman believers he wrote, "How beautiful are the feet of those who preach good news" (Romans 10:15). For Paul, those who were ready to go to war against the spirit of the age had their shoes of service on and were ready to march.

Sacrificial ministry to others can include such activities as community service to your neighborhood, serving in your local church, public service in government, and, of course, evangelism and missions. Sacrificial service is the exercise of giving Jesus to the world. Service stands in stark contrast to the get-all-you-can-get-for-yourself spirit of the age. Believers who battle for holiness will look different from nonbelievers. We don't live for ourselves. We don't even belong to ourselves. We are called to give our lives, our love, our earthly goods, our strength, and our friendship to serve the world.

Dr. C. Everett Koop, former surgeon general of the United States, has distinguished himself as a godly man and a servant of people. In three decades of service at Philadelphia's Children's Hospital, Dr. Koop treated over 100,000 pediatric patients, many of them small enough to hold in one hand. Koop pioneered many techniques for saving the lives of malformed and premature babies. He treated countless numbers of deformed infants that other physicians wouldn't touch. One of his patients, who needed 37 facial and abdominal surgeries to correct birth defects, is now a university graduate. Another patient, for whom Dr. Koop fashioned a new esophagus out of a section of colon, went on to become a pediatric surgeon.[2]

As surgeon general, Dr. Koop became America's family doctor. Though his career was surrounded by controversy, Dr. Koop came to be respected as a man of great integrity. "To a jaded general public hungry for integrity in their leaders, Koop became a genuine folk hero."[3] Though Koop was often the bearer of bad news about cancer and AIDS, the public trusted him because they knew he was concerned for their health.

Sacrificial service, as exemplified by Dr. Koop, comes against the pleasure-oriented, self-indulgent spirit of the age that permeates our society. I talk to pastors all over the nation who cannot motivate their people to sacrificial service. Many Christians insist, "My time, my money, and my energy are mine to use as I please. What right does my pastor have to tell me what to do?" They are caught up in the spirit of the age. They have adopted the attitude of the world. Holiness in a fallen world doesn't mean that we retreat to the desert of selfishness. It means that we go into the world to bring the gospel of peace to those who so desperately need it.

Fortified with Faith

It's easy to become pessimistic in a world of so many problems. Satan wants to impress us with his power. He wants us to see all the violence and crime in our cities and be filled with despair. He calls our attention to carnal, backslidden Christian leaders and tempts us to cynicism. When we feel hopeless for our cities and do nothing as a result, Satan wins. When we see poverty and injustice rampant in the world and retreat into our own little world saying, "There's nothing I can do anyway," he defeats us.

God has provided a weapon to defuse Satan's fiery darts of pessimism, discouragement, and disillusionment. We are to lift up the shield of faith (Ephesians 6:16). Satan wants to impress us with his power in order to produce unbelief in our hearts. Unbelief paralyzes Christians. It keeps us from sacrificial service and wholehearted trust in the Lord. Don't be overawed with sin! Lift up the shield of faith and quench the darts of disbelief.

The importance of the shield of faith was brought home to me in a dramatic way during a prayer meeting in Amsterdam several years ago. Amsterdam was the pornography capital of Europe at that time, shipping almost $1 billion worth of child porn into the United States every year. Our city was also the largest center for homosexuals on the continent. There were almost 12,000 hard drug users in the city and somewhere between 12,000–15,000 prostitutes working in and around Amsterdam's red-light district, an area 6 blocks wide and 12 blocks long.

That night we were focusing our prayers on the red-light district. In the middle of the meeting my friend Joy Dawson interrupted me and asked if she could say something. She is a Bible teacher from New Zealand who was visiting the city to give a series of lectures on revival. I asked her to share with us what was on her heart.

She stood and solemnly announced, "I have never attended a prayer meeting where the prayers reflected so much unbelief. You dear people are more impressed with the power of sin in Amsterdam than you are with God's power to conquer sin. Your prayers sound very nice, but your hearts don't believe that God is going to change this city."

As Joy shared her conviction with us I realized that she was right! We were in a spiritual battle for the city, but we prayed like we were losing. Satan had launched his fiery darts at us to discourage us and defeat us, and he had scored a direct hit.

After Joy confronted us, we repented of our unbelief. I remember asking the Lord to forgive me for letting down the shield of faith and giving the devil a clear target. From that moment on I refused to be impressed with sin or with Satan's power. I chose instead to be impressed with God! He is all-powerful. He is infinite in His greatness and goodness. There is no limit to what He can do if we believe Him and open our hearts to Him.

We must not give in to the unbelief and cynicism of the spirit of the age. We must lift up the shield of faith by believing deep in our hearts that there is no problem too great for God. We maintain an attitude of faith by worshiping God and focusing on His character regardless of the circumstances. Faith grows in our hearts through worship and prayer. We get rid of unbelief by treating it as sin—which is what it is. We must confess our unbelief and ask God to forgive us for it.

Constant Communication

When army troops advance into enemy territory during war time, they go to extraordinary lengths to maintain their lines of communication. Enemy forces can score an important victory if they can cut off communication between headquarters and the troops on the front line. Being surrounded in hostile territory and unable to communicate with your commanding officer can be disastrous. Defeat is certain.

The last weapon I will mention for fighting the good fight is prayer. Prayer is our supply line to God. Paul admonished us, "Pray at all times in the Spirit, with all prayer and supplication" (Ephesians 6:18). Without continuous communication with our "commanding officer" we are doomed to be overwhelmed by the spirit of the age. God is our source of wisdom for operating in this hostile world.

It is vital that we stay in touch with Him in order to know what to do. He is committed to our victory over the spirit of the age, but He cannot help us if we don't stay close to Him through prayer.

Prayer helps us discern when the enemy is seeking to seduce us away from our devotion to Jesus. When we are in communication with God, He can alert us of Satan's attempts to undermine our faith and love for truth.

It was prayer that helped us discern and disarm a subtle attack of the enemy in Amsterdam. Sally and I led an evangelistic team in the red-light district for several years. During a stretch of several months, every woman on our team who lived in that neighborhood came under some form of depression. After much fasting and prayer we believed we had discerned a particular strategy against our workers that went beyond normal explanation. We became convinced that it was a spiritual attack to discourage our workers and close down our ministry to the prostitutes.

After many months of concerted prayer, faith grew in our hearts enabling us to trust God for victory over the depression our women team members were experiencing. The attack was broken. Had we not been in constant communication with the Lord, we might never have discerned the root of the problem and deflected Satan's attack. Without prayer, our ministry among the prostitutes of Amsterdam probably would have shut down. Prayer is absolutely essential to winning the victory over the spirit of the age.

Fighting to Win

I learned an important principle for spiritual warfare in Amsterdam while working with men and women who were dependent on chemical substances. Addicts could not be helped unless they were desperate. I would often asked them, "Are you a junkie, or do you think you can get yourself out of this mess?" If they denied being hooked, or if they thought they could somehow kick the habit themselves, they were helpless. Junkies could never be set free if they didn't admit their need for help and fight the fight on God's terms.

So it is in our battle for holiness against the spirit of the age. We can win the battle, but it won't happen until we are ready to fight and are convinced of our total dependence on God for the victory.

I heard a friend speak recently, and he told the story of three men who were working on a pile of rocks. Each man was asked what he was doing. One said, "Shaping a stone." The second replied, "Building a wall." The last man responded with great exuberance, "I'm carving stones to build a cathedral to the glory of God!"

The faith and vision of the third man is our example. Some Christians may view their day-to-day experience as a struggle for survival in a hostile world. It's more than a struggle; it's a war. But we can win the battle. In fact, the battle has already been won. We are simply in the process of claiming on a day-to-day basis what the Lord Jesus has already secured on the cross.

In our fight for holiness against the spirit of the age we are continuing the work of the saints of ages past in building a great cathedral to the glory of God. God is the architect; He has shown us how to build. Paul wrote, "According to the commission of God given to me, like a skilled master builder I laid a foundation, and another man is building upon it. Let each man take care how he builds upon it. For no other foundation can any one lay than that which is laid, which is Jesus Christ" (1 Corinthians 3:10,11). The foundation, the Lord Jesus, is in place. Paul and others God used as instruments to convey His Word have prepared the blueprint. And believers through the centuries have been called to take their place as "living stones" (1 Peter 2:5) in God's temple by living in holiness.

The cathedral is not constructed without a struggle, however. Paul continues, "Each man's work will become manifest; for the Day will disclose it, because it will be revealed with fire, and the fire will test what sort of work each one has done" (1 Corinthians 3:13). Yet we have God's promise that His protection attends us as we fight against the fiery darts of Satan and the oppression of spirit of the age: "Do you not know that you are God's temple and that God's Spirit dwells in you. If anyone destroys God's temple, God will destroy him" (1 Corinthians 16,17). We can fight the good fight with the confidence that victory is assured.

In the early 1950s two men stood in a field bordered by acres of orange groves in southern California. Walter turned to Arthur and said, "Some day I would like to build a park here for people's enjoyment. If I do that, I think the property around it will become very valuable. I encourage you to buy all the land in this area you can."

"Are you crazy?" Arthur responded. "People won't drive 25 miles from Los Angeles through all these orange groves to go to a park!"

To his great regret, Art Linkletter did not take the advice of his friend, Walt Disney. He scorned the opportunity of a lifetime to own acreage in Orange County, California, which is now worth hundreds of millions of dollars because it borders Walt's "park," Disneyland.

The opportunity God offers us today is infinitely more valuable than the offer Walt Disney made to Art Linkletter. God holds out to us great blessings in a hostile world governed by the spirit of the age. He promises us daily victory in a battle He has already won. He calls us to participate in a dream much bigger than the glittery American dream. All that's needed to activate these benefits is our commitment to be His holy people. It's an offer too good to refuse.

Floyd and Sally McClung, and their two children Misha and Matthew, work with Youth With A Mission. They are based in Amsterdam, Holland, but travel the world preaching and teaching. For more information about their ministry write to:

Youth With A Mission
4931 Lori Ann
Irvine, California 92714.

Notes

CHAPTER 1

1. Jerry Bridges, *The Practice of Godliness* (Colorado Springs: Navpress, 1983), p. 148.
2. Bob Goudzwaard, *Idols of Our Time* (Downers Grove, IL: InterVarsity Press, 1984), p. 12.

CHAPTER 2

1. Charles Colson, *Against the Night* (Ann Arbor, MI: Servant Publications, 1989), p. 11.
2. Quoted from Alexander Solzhenitsyn, *From Under the Rubble* (Washington, D.C.: Gateway Editions, 1981), p. 105.

CHAPTER 3

1. Lyndall Clarke, *More* magazine (New Zealand), pp. 90-93, (date unknown).
2. Anastasia Toufexis, *Our Violent Kids; Time* magazine, June 12, 1989, p. 54.

CHAPTER 4

1. Quoted in Charles Colson, *Against the Night* (Ann Arbor, MI: Servant Publications, 1989), p. 139.

CHAPTER 8

1. Will Durant, *The Story of Philosophy* (New York: Washington Square Press, 1964), p. 231.
2. Quoted in Charles Colson, *Against the Night* (Ann Arbor, MI: Servant Publications, 1989), p. 29.

CHAPTER 9

1. Richard W. Fox and T. Jackson Lears, eds., *The Culture of Consumption* (New York: Pantheon Books, 1983), p. 4.
2. Ibid, p. 4.
3. John F. Kavanaugh, *Following Christ in a Consumer Society* (Maryknoll, NY: Orbis Books, 1981), p. 21.

CHAPTER 10

1. Os Guinness, *The Gravedigger File* (Downers Grove, IL: InterVarsity Press, 1983), p. 94.
2. Ibid, p. 96.
3. Quoted in Guinness, *The Gravedigger File*, p. 103.

CHAPTER 11

1. Os Guinness, *The Gravedigger File* (Downers Grove, IL: InterVarsity Press, 1983), p. 51.

CHAPTER 12

1. Jerry Bridges, *The Practice of Godliness* (Colorado Springs: NavPress, 1983), p. 149.

CHAPTER 13

1. Jerry Bridges, *The Practice of Godliness* (Colorado Springs: Navpress, 1983), p. 24.
2. Ibid, p. 37.

CHAPTER 14

1. C.S. Lewis, *Mere Christianity* (New York: MacMillan, 1964), pp. 110-11.

CHAPTER 15

1. Quoted in L.E. Maxwell, *Born Crucified* (Chicago: Moody Press, 1973), pp. 55-7.

CHAPTER 17

1. Daniel Q. Haney, "It May Not Be Shocking but People Tell Lies for Sex," *The Desert Sun*, March 15, 1990.
2. Philip Yancey, *The Embattled Career of Dr. Koop., Christianity Today*, October 20, 1989, p. 18.
3. Ibid, p. 19.

The Father Heart of God

God Loves You—
Learn to Know His
Compassionate Touch

by Floyd McClung

The Father Heart of God is a book about the healing power of God's love. The author richly illustrates how the loving, compassionate Father heart of God enables us to overcome insecurity and the devastating effects of some of life's most painful experiences.

Balanced teaching on human responsibility and God's love is presented in practical examples. You will discover new ways to: overcome disappointment; win over insecurity; restore broken relationships; and defeat pride—and through it all experience the healing power of God's love.